HOW TO READ
GARDENS

HOW TO READ
GARDENS

A crash course in garden appreciation

HERBERT PRESS
LONDON

Lorraine Harrison

First published in Great Britain in 2010 by
HERBERT PRESS
An imprint of A&C Black Publishers Limited
36 Soho Square
London W1D 3QY, UK
www.acblack.com

ISBN: 978-1-4081-2837-4

A CIP catalogue record for this book
is available from the British Library

Colour origination by Ivy Press Reprographics
Printed in China

This book was conceived, designed
and produced by

Ivy Press

210 High Street
Lewes, East Sussex
BN7 2NS, UK
www.ivy-group.co.uk

CREATIVE DIRECTOR Peter Bridgewater
PUBLISHER Jason Hook
EDITORIAL DIRECTOR Caroline Earle
ART DIRECTOR Michael Whitehead
PROJECT EDITOR Stephanie Evans
DESIGN JC Lanaway
ILLUSTRATIONS Coral Mula
PICTURE MANAGER Katie Greenwood

Cover images: Corbis/Michael Boys (top);
Eric Crichton (bottom).

Contents

Foreword

I have been lucky enough to have grown up in a famous, much-visited garden but Sissinghurst remains very personal to me. Although I have known the garden all my life, I have not found a more beautiful place than the White Garden by moonlight. Since the age of six, when I was small enough to run my hand along the feathery tops of the box hedges, I have loved the smell, touch, sight and sheer sensibility of this enclosed space.

My grandparents' joint horticultural achievement, with Harold Nicolson responsible for the layout, and Vita Sackville-West for the planting, has been an inspiration for gardeners all over the world. Sissinghurst is a place full of surprises, with its series of garden rooms, often devoted to a particular colour or a particular flowering season. The beauty of getting to know any garden is like re-reading a much-loved book. One looks forward to returning to familiar pages, and to lingering over well-loved passages as well as discovering new and different perspectives that have somehow never occurred to one before. So a book entitled How to Read Gardens *is apt* indeed, acting as a friendly personal guide to accompany visitors on a tour of any garden, historic or modern, public or private. The expert eye of its author shows garden lovers how to enhance their appreciation of a visit by reading the visual clues laid out before them.

My father always compared the flowering season at Sissinghurst to a five-act play, and there is a writing desk in the South Cottage at Sissinghurst that looks directly out onto the oranges, yellows and reds of the Cottage Garden, affording a front-row view of this annual drama as the evolving play is enacted through the window for the lucky occupant within. Beginning quietly in February when a few snowdrops push up out of the earth, this lovely garden drama slowly develops. The vivid green beauty of the spring is followed by the full rosy glory of high summer, and the play concludes with a final autumnal burst of colour before closing down to winter quietness once again.

JULIET NICOLSON, January 2010

Werribee Park, Melbourne, Australia

The ornamental parterre and manicured lawns were two European garden styles used to grace the grounds of the 19th-century mansion built outside Melbourne by Thomas and Andrew Chirnside.

Garden visiting has never been so popular, but how many of us really understand what we are looking at when strolling through a beautiful garden? Is it an original landscape or a re-creation? Is the planting material authentic or composed of modern hybrids? Are the steps and terracing in the Italianate style or Arts and Crafts? And what is that apparent ruin spied through the trees?

The truth is that most gardens of any age are like a palimpsest: successive generations have changed, adapted and influenced the soft and hard fabric of the place over time. Inevitably many of the gardens we wander through

today are an amalgam of changing fashions and social circumstance. Garden landscapes can record the rise and fall of a family's fortunes, record the human exploratory spirit through the introduction of foreign plant species, and display several lifetimes of endeavour in making a piece of land quite unique and personal.

How to Read Gardens is a crash course in garden visiting, rather than a chronological history of garden making. Used as a field guide it will help you to spot and identify historical influences, origins and styles as well as the odd flight of fancy. Photographs of gardens from many cultures and countries provide a taste of the wealth and variety of places to visit, while detailed illustrations show generic examples of features and details to look out for in individual gardens. This combination equips you with a visual language with which to interpret and understand the many disparate elements that make a garden.

The aim of the book is to provide you with the knowledge you need to tease out the clues that will tell the story of a garden's past. From the grandest estate to the smallest suburban patch, *How to Read Gardens* will enliven, inform and, most importantly, increase the pleasure of your every future garden visit.

Roses everywhere
Roses, whether hybrids grown for their glorious colour and long flowering or old-fashioned varieties for their intoxicating scent, continue to have an enduring appeal.

History of Garden Visiting

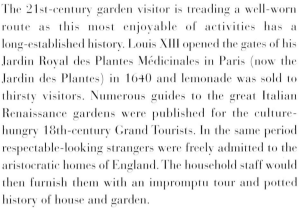

The 21st-century garden visitor is treading a well-worn route as this most enjoyable of activities has a long-established history. Louis XIII opened the gates of his Jardin Royal des Plantes Médicinales in Paris (now the Jardin des Plantes) in 1640 and lemonade was sold to thirsty visitors. Numerous guides to the great Italian Renaissance gardens were published for the culture-hungry 18th-century Grand Tourists. In the same period respectable-looking strangers were freely admitted to the aristocratic homes of England. The household staff would then furnish them with an impromptu tour and potted history of house and garden.

Today the range of gardens open to the public varies from the grandest historical site, owned, managed and administered by teams of historical and horticultural experts, to a small private plot whose gardening-crazy owner generously throws open his or her gate for a few days a year in aid of a charitable cause. The range of visitors is almost as diverse as the gardens themselves and includes plant experts, architectural historians, dilettantes and casual strollers – just as in the past.

Perhaps inevitably some very special gardens have become victims of their own success. (The Alhambra in Spain and Sissinghurst Castle in England spring readily to mind.) The price we pay for entry to see these truly wonderful places is a loss of atmosphere, and the deterioration of the very turf beneath our feet, as we share the experience with so many others. Therefore consider a gentle plea to include some of the more modest and less

The fruit of the lemon
Citrus trees became within reach of wealthy 19th-century garden owners in temperate climes who could afford to build and maintain specialist glasshouses.

well-known (though often just as inspiring) gardens on your itinerary, alongside the more usual and famous.

Apart from wear and tear, another impact of the sheer volume of garden visitors is the way the route by which a garden is seen has to be managed. Do be aware of how a garden would originally have been approached and viewed, as this was always a carefully orchestrated and considered element in planning a garden. Sadly far too often the demands of café, shop and ticket booths have subverted the original grand plan!

Burnett Memorial, Central Park, New York, USA
The Conservatory Garden is the only formal part of Central Park. Its bronze fountain memorialises children's book author Frances Hodgson Burnett.

Dating a Garden

The often-vexed question of attributing a date to a garden is one that can perplex even the most knowledgeable garden historian. So much of a garden is formed from mutable materials such as trees, plants and water that it never reaches a point at which it is finished, complete. A garden is constantly in a state of change and flux as plants grow, develop with the seasons, respond to the climate, then eventually and inevitably die. Add to this the intervention of successive owners with their changing needs and fashions and the problem is further compounded!

The earliest existent records of a garden layout are Ancient Egyptian and date from before 2000 BC although this does not, of course, mean there were no gardens prior to this period. Imagine the number of variations on what we recognise as 'the garden' that have emerged over the centuries, and in so many regions of the world, and the

Pleasure gardens
Over the centuries gardens have been appreciated as places for leisure, pleasure and quiet contemplation.

problem of setting a date to a garden becomes ever more apparent. To simplify the issue, look hard at a garden and ask yourself: is this new? If not, how long has a garden been on this site? If it adheres to a strict historical scheme does it originate from the period or is it a later re-creation? Has this garden evolved over time, incorporating different stylistic influences?

In truth garden makers are a promiscuous lot and have shamelessly borrowed and adapted elements and styles from a multitude of periods and places, often with little concern for consistency. Few gardens are 'pure and unadulterated' in this sense. Even contemporary viewers could be unsure of a garden's provenance. The term the French used for the 18th-century English landscape park, referring to it as the *anglo-chinois* style, is a perfect illustration of this confusion!

Remember also that artistry of effect, or horticultural excellence, is often of far greater importance to a garden maker than historical accuracy. It is not uncommon to find modern plant hybrids clothing the bones of a 17th-century garden layout. This seeming disregard is not always due to lack of attention or care; the original planting list may not have survived or, if it has, the varieties may no longer exist. Perhaps *How to Read Gardens* will make visitors aware of the many historical and stylistic trends evident in gardens without becoming overly concerned about authenticity as, by their very nature, gardens are living and changing entities. Above all, enjoy and appreciate all the gardens you visit, whatever their age!

Ornamental urn
In a grand garden the style and choice of materials used for ornaments are often dictated by the age and architecture of the main house.

What Is It For?

Introduction

Gardens are created for a great number of reasons, not all of them practical or sensual, and the range of garden types often confounds and confuses the visitor. The purpose of a garden profoundly affects its appearance, so one of the first questions to ask on arrival is 'What is this garden for? Why is it here?' Gardens fulfil many different functions: they can display wealth, power and status; they may express theological and philosophical ideas; some produce food or medicine; others are repositories of scientific knowledge; and, of course, many gardens simply give immense pleasure just by looking and smelling beautiful.

Palm House, Schönbrunn Palace Gardens, Vienna, Austria

The great botanical gardens of the world are hothouses of scientific endeavour. Think of them as the museums and universities of the horticultural world, their enormous glass domes housing rare and precious plants, all of major ecological importance.

Munstead Wood, Surrey, England

The traditional English country house garden has become a classic style that is much copied, its mood conducive to relaxation, entertainment and recreation. The layout of the garden relates closely to the house and the planting is less formal.

Nitobe Memorial Garden, Vancouver, Canada

The ethos and style of Japanese gardens are influential in many countries. Themed spaces are frequently incorporated within larger garden schemes such as parks or arboreta. They offer a change of atmosphere and add a new visual sensibility.

Felbrigg Hall, Norfolk, England

Although often very attractive, the main function of a vegetable, fruit or herb garden is to supply food or medicine. Such spaces are primarily hard-working areas of production, rather than public displays intended to delight or impress visitors.

Gardens of Grandeur

Just like the buildings they surround, the grand gardens of palaces, seats of government and large private residences are designed to impress, excite and even intimidate the viewer. (Ask yourself, do you feel *comfortable* in such spaces?) Using a carefully orchestrated set of garden elements, they exude wealth, power and status. Size frequently does matter in conveying social position so always consider the full extent of a garden. Because land is expensive and often scarce, only the rich can afford to turn precious farm or building land into beautiful gardens.

Villa d'Este, Tivoli, Italy
Note the scale, complexity and sophisticated design of the great Italian Renaissance gardens, all of them the exact antithesis of the small domestic plot.

The entrance
The approach to a building of status is paramount and the garden plays a key role here. Look out for obvious clues such as gatehouses, lodges, ornate gates decorated with coats of arms, and, beyond these architectural elements, long avenues of trees, framing the drive.

Labour
Grand gardens require small armies of people to maintain them. The upkeep of large areas of well-tended lawns and elaborately planted flower borders is very labour-intensive and requires a high level of expertise. A considerable workforce is another visible sign of wealth.

Function

A romantic ruin may look intriguing and attractive but serve no practical purpose. However, a pavilion may be pretty but also provide shelter from the elements, so is functional too. The greater the number of 'useless' features in a property, the wealthier its owner.

Ornament

Note the quality and quantity of ornamental and decorative features in a garden. Fine sculpture, well-built structures, functioning fountains, unusual urns, purpose-built furniture all denote that a high degree of care, attention and expense has been lavished on the garden.

Gardens for Pleasure

Powerscourt, County Wicklow, Ireland

A leisurely stroll through a beautiful garden or park is as popular today as in previous eras, the need for open green space, an arresting view and clean, fresh air an enduring desire.

The pleasure garden or pleasure ground was popular in Europe from the mid-18th century onwards. Such spaces are all about social interaction and enjoyment. A certain informality of layout and planting and eclectic building styles frequently characterise gardens that are intended to please and divert. Areas for musical recitals, the playing of games, taking refreshments and, most importantly, promenading all feature. The idea was fully democratised in the 19th century with the creation of public parks, and the notion of designated public spaces still holds currency throughout the world today.

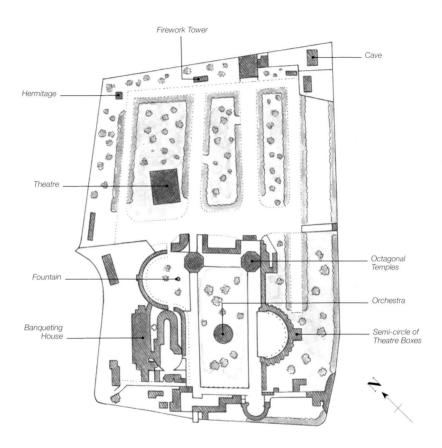

Firework Tower

Cave

Hermitage

Theatre

Octagonal
Temples

Fountain

Orchestra

Banqueting
House

Semi-circle of
Theatre Boxes

N

**Plan of Vauxhall Gardens,
London, England, 1826**

Vauxhall Gardens was a commercial pleasure garden that flourished in London from *c.*1661–1859. In many ways it set a template for subsequent public spaces. For a modest entrance fee a cross-section of society gathered to enjoy diverse entertainments. Families and friends strolled amid flower beds, picnicked on lawns or ate more formally in special theatre-style boxes. Musical, theatrical and circus-style performances were especially popular, as were the spectacular firework displays, and all of it enjoyed against the backdrop of a garden setting.

21

Country Retreats

The Garden House, Devon, England
In a controlled and sometimes rather contrived way, the style of the country house garden aims to complement and echo the appearance of the natural landscape beyond its boundaries.

The concept of having 'a place in the country' crosses time and continents but it is the 19th-century English country house, and its accompanying garden, that best typifies the ideal. Industrialisation consumed land and, in the eyes of many, the contrasting countryside became imbued with superior moral qualities. The wealthy bought or built substantial country retreats, surrounding them with relaxed gardens in which to play, entertain and be closer to nature. Note how house and garden relate, often the same palette of vernacular materials is used for each. Planting is less formal, with native species used freely.

Views

The surrounding landscape is invited into the garden, often by the device of the 'borrowed view'. Garden and nature appear merged rather than sharply demarcated one from the other by high walls, hedges or fences, as in the town.

Entertaining

Social rules are more relaxed in the country; just as clothes are less formal so too are gardens. Outdoor eating is popular, areas for tables and chairs abundant, often sited on generous terraces close to the house with ample comfortable chairs.

Games

Country house parties revolved around pleasure and play. You will see numerous areas dedicated to games, such as tennis courts, croquet lawns and bowling greens as well as extensive shrubberies for strolling. Smart stabling for horses or garaging for cars may also feature.

Rusticity

Decoration is often more playful in the country house garden than on a more formally designed estate. Rustic-style buildings, furniture and fencing seem especially fitting in country settings. You may see more use of wood and brick for architectural features than stone.

Domestic Gardens

Domestic gardens come in all shapes but not in all sizes: most are small and some may be little more than a balcony, backyard or roof terrace. Issues of security, privacy and propriety mean that their boundaries frequently act as a barrier against the world beyond. Smart courtyard gardens can be exemplary exercises in tasteful restraint while family gardens often suffer from the demands of fulfilling too many functions, simultaneously housing a child's play area, rabbit hutch, fish pond, greenhouse, shed, vegetable patch, plus the occasional flower and shrub!

Small but beautiful
Where space is at a premium, less is definitely more. As shown here, the restrained and somewhat minimalist design approach works particularly well in courtyard gardens.

Space

Small gardens encourage the use of vertical spaces, and plants such as roses and fuchsias are often grown as standards as a way of using less ground as well as adding height and interest. For the same reason climbers are grown up trellis and pergolas.

Plants

Look for a sense of unity and purpose in a small garden. Note how a limited use of flowers set against a background structure of evergreens imparts a sense of tranquillity, while a layering of large architectural leaves provides structure.

Detail

Common garden elements such as gates, fences, edgings, furniture and plant pots are rarely bespoke (as they often are in large-scale gardens) but mass-produced and sold in their thousands. You will spot recurring designs such as this gate, once very popular in British suburbs.

Ornaments

Domestic garden makers often feel less bound by tradition than their grander neighbours, and this can result in a charming, if eclectic, mix of ornamental and decorative styles. Do not be surprised to encounter a seated gnome alongside a recumbent Buddha!

Islamic Gardens

The model of the Islamic garden dates back to pre-Islamic Persia. It is common throughout the Middle East and Asia as well as North Africa, Spain and Turkey. Its strict geometric design has become a fundamental paradigm and you will see its influence in countless gardens across the world. Conceived literally as a 'paradise on earth', these tranquil enclosed spaces were originally an oasis of cool and green, offering protection from marauding animals and desert heat. They are more about architecture and control than nature, characterised by pools, rills, fountains and shade-giving pavilions.

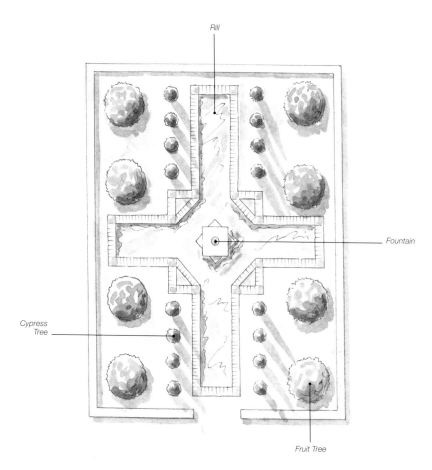

Rill

Fountain

Cypress
Tree

Fruit Tree

Islamic garden plan

The classic Islamic garden is surrounded by high walls, and the interior space is divided by four rills or channels of water. These converge in a central pool, often with a fountain. Such gardens are called *charbagh*, in which the water channels represent the four rivers of life – milk, honey, water and wine – flowing through paradise. Star and octagonal motifs are emblems of life and the intellect. Tall, narrow evergreen trees, most commonly cypress, are symbolic of mortality. These, along with fruit trees, provide shade.

Gardens of Meaning

Like Islamic gardens, Japanese or Zen gardens represent 'heaven on earth' and are redolent of deep philosophical and symbolic meanings. Visually very distinctive, they have a pared-down simplicity in which plants are subordinate to structural elements. The function of such gardens is intellectual and meditative rather than sensual, their balance, harmony and serenity conducive to introspection and silent reflection. Rocks, water, gravel and plants are arranged to create miniature landscapes in which space becomes deceptive. A sense of scale dissolves when contemplating such a scene.

Nazen-ji, Kyoto, Japan
In this Karesansui, or dry landscape garden, the gravel raked in straight lines represents still water whilst the raked curves symbolise more turbulent waves.

Rock
Hard elements such as rock, stone and gravel are key in such gardens. Carefully positioned rocks represent strength, purity and permanence. Gravel is raked to mimic ripples of water. Look for stone paths that meander gently through areas of moss.

Water
You will always see a water feature in a true Japanese garden, usually brimming with fish. Pools, streams and waterfalls are all symbolic of the passage of time. A simple bridge marks the crossing from one world to the next.

Plants

Note how the colour range of plants is restricted primarily to evergreens, except in autumn when specimen trees such as acers blaze into colour. The shapes and sizes of trees are constantly controlled, as with this evergreen, pruned to resemble clouds.

Ornament

Stone lanterns were traditionally used to light the way for guests at evening tea ceremonies. They are placed where illumination is most needed in the garden such as at a gate, by a bridge or where a path changes direction.

Secret Gardens

St-Paul-de-Mausole, St-Rémy-Provence, France

The symbolic ideal of the enclosed garden is alluded to in the Old Testament's Song of Solomon: 'A garden enclosed is my sister, my spouse: a spring shut up, a fountain sealed.'

Known variously as a *hortus conclusus* (Latin: enclosed garden) or *giardino segreto* (Italian: secret garden) these enclosed gardens are full of Christian and literary symbolism. Alluding to the Virgin Mary, whose virginity made her enclosed and complete, they are traditionally associated with privacy and the protection of women. Not all such gardens remained so high minded and they increasingly became places of pleasure and diversion, their hidden nature perfect for secret assignations. As smaller retreats set within larger gardens, they are a precursor to the garden room.

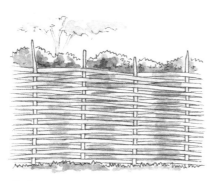

Enclosure

Privacy is provided by walls, hedges, fences or, occasionally, more open trellis-work or woven wattle fencing. All of these structures screen the garden's occupants from the world outside and also create a microclimate for growing tender plants.

Seats

The secret garden is furnished with shaded places to sit, often under leafy bowers. Turf seats were popular in the medieval period. A stone or wooden seat is planted with grass or sweet-smelling herbs such as camomile or thyme.

Plants

Plants are often chosen for their symbolic meaning. The white Madonna lily, *Lilium candidum*, represents purity and in religious paintings the Angel Gabriel is depicted holding a lily at the Annunciation. In contrast red roses symbolise the blood of Christian martyrs.

Cloister gardens

Convent and monastery cloister gardens, in which an arched covered colonnade encloses a square or rectangular garden, relate closely to the concept behind the *hortus conclusus*. These peaceful spaces are sometimes planted with herbs for medicinal use.

Gardens of Ideas

Some gardens express ideas on philosophy, politics, poetry and even science. Such intellectually driven spaces are exclusive, speaking only to those who understand the allusions being made. In no other type of garden is it more important to ask the questions 'What is this and why has it been placed here: what does it convey?' For example, within the main garden at Stowe, Buckinghamshire, England, William Kent (1686–1748) placed classically inspired structures that celebrated the virtues of the antique, while those positioned in the landscape beyond were gothic in style, alluding to native Saxon traditions.

Garden of Cosmic Speculation, Dumfries, Scotland

Architectural theorist Charles Jencks (b. 1939) has created a spectacular garden at Portrack House in which he explores such complex ideas as the substance of the universe and chaos theory.

Setting

Ideology in gardens is rarely encumbered with floral decoration. Sparse landscape settings provide the perfect foil for structures that convey meaning such as these inscribed stone tablets at Little Sparta, Dunsyre, Scotland. Where planting does occur, it is usually wild or informal.

Nomenclature

Clues to meaning lie in the naming of parts in such gardens. In the landscaped gardens of Stowe, Buckinghamshire, England, the Temple of British Worthies is placed in a valley called the Elysian Fields, which in Greek mythology was the last resting place for the souls of the virtuous.

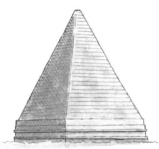

Style

Style is a key element in the narrative
of these gardens. At Castle Howard in
North Yorkshire, England, three ancient
civilisations are represented architecturally:
the Mausoleum is Grecian, the Pyramid
Egyptian and the Temple of the Four
Winds is Roman.

Meaning

Be aware that superficial appearances can
be deceptive. This Temple of Philosophy
at Château d'Ermenonville, Oise, France,
is unfinished but it is not a garden ruin in
the traditional sense. Instead its unfinished
state speaks of the incompleteness of
human knowledge.

Healing Gardens

Traditional physic and herb gardens are some of the most attractive gardens one can visit, yet are also the most productive and useful. Herbs have been grown for their medicinal, culinary and domestic uses for centuries, the earliest herbals (written guides to their use) are from ancient China. Often attached to religious establishments, physic gardens are closely allied to the development of botany. Medieval monks grew herbs in simply arranged geometric beds but later secular examples became more decorative. Many large gardens still have areas devoted to their cultivation.

Layout

Herbs are commonly grown in geometric patterns of varying complexity. By the 15th and 16th centuries elaborate knot designs were popular in the west, formed by low clipped hedges of lavender and germander, although you are more likely to see the more permanent box (*Buxus*) used today.

Identification

If you spot a bed full of neatly arranged and well-identified plants it is quite likely to be a herb garden. Originally, these were gardens with a practical purpose: a physician in search of a remedy or cure would need to find and identify a plant quickly and accurately.

Containers

Gardeners frequently grow herbs in containers, just as the Romans did. Many herb species originate from the Far East and Mediterranean regions so are particularly suited to being grown in free-draining pots, and tender varieties can be easily moved indoors in winter.

Beds

Herbs have traditionally been cultivated in raised beds as this helps separate medicinal herbs from those grown for culinary purposes. Timber or brick may be used, although woven wattle fencing is particularly appropriate for re-creations of medieval-style herb gardens.

Fruitful Gardens

Many fruit and vegetable gardens lie hidden behind high walls some distance away from the main dwelling. Traditionally any area devoted to a utilitarian purpose in a garden such as growing fruit, vegetables or cut flowers was shielded from view. Apart from matters of propriety, towering walls had the added benefit of creating favourable microclimates. Fashions change, however, and the *potager* style of vegetable-growing became popular whereby productive and decorative plants are cultivated alongside each other in patterned arrangements, providing visual as well as culinary pleasure.

Normanby Hall, Lincolnshire, England
Here the ordered layout of beds and the utilitarian arrangement of paths and buildings is typical of a 19th-century walled kitchen garden.

Enclosure

Productive gardens look beautiful during the summer months but empty and sad for much of the rest of the year, hence the development of the kitchen garden screened behind brick walls. Many former kitchen gardens have undergone extensive restoration in recent times.

Buildings

Running a productive kitchen garden requires manpower and equipment so you will always find a range of buildings attached to or in the vicinity of the garden, such as tool and potting sheds, while tender tropical fruits require specialist conditions provided by glasshouses.

Layout

For maximum efficiency the extensive kitchen garden should be a model of order, organised to a strict geometric plan. In 18th-century Europe, when the fashion was for rolling, open landscapes, kitchen gardens became enclosed havens of production and industry.

Paths

Note how vegetable gardens are always intersected by several paths; access is required for efficient cultivation and paths must be of sufficient width to allow a gardener to push a wheelbarrow along them with ease. These are primarily working gardens, not places of idle pleasure!

Botanical Gardens

Great botanical gardens are found throughout the world. They have a long history: Aristotle had his own botanical garden in the third century BC. The first European garden of this type was established in Pisa, Italy, in 1543, and others quickly followed across the Continent. Botanical gardens have played vital roles in the development of medicine and international trade. Though a joy to visit, their primary function is to identify, classify and preserve botanical material from around the world. From these centres of horticultural expertise, knowledge is freely shared and exchanged internationally.

Botanical Garden, Padua, Italy
Created in 1545 for the study of medicinal plants, the garden retains its circular central layout, symbolising the world. The high wall was built to prevent night-time raids on its precious plant material.

Glasshouses
The most ubiquitous, not to say impressive, feature of the botanical garden is the specialist glasshouse. Their height allows tall specimen trees such as palms to grow freely, while the extensive glazing affords maximum light. Temperature and humidity can also be carefully controlled to re-create tropical or subtropical conditions.

Exotics
You will notice that well-labelled groups of non-native trees and shrubs abound in botanical gardens. Such gardens are, after all, collections of living exhibits. Even today, when imported exotic species are more commonplace in our homes and gardens, you are quite likely to encounter a plant you have not seen before.

Plants

During the 18th and 19th centuries botanical gardens sponsored major plant-hunting expeditions all over the world. Many of the exotic species brought back by collectors, among them rhododendrons and azaleas, profoundly affect the way our public and private gardens look today.

Herbaria

Along with extensive libraries, botanical institutions often have herbaria. These are systematically arranged collections of plants, whole or in part, which have been preserved, most usually by drying and pressing. The Royal Botanic Gardens, Kew, England, alone has over seven million pressed plants.

The Collectors

**Westonbirt,
Gloucestershire,
England**
In Britain arboreta
began to be planted
in the 17th century.
Westonbirt, which
dates from the late
1820s, forms part
of The National
Arboreta and is
open to the public.

You will find plant collections in many different forms. The largest are the great public and private plant collections of trees known as arboreta, and their cousins the pinetum (conifers), the fruticetum (shrubs) and the viticetum (vines). Their prime aim is the collection and categorisation of plant species but aesthetic consideration is often given to their grouping in a parkland setting. Historically such collections denote wealth with tailor-made glasshouses constructed to cultivate individual species brought back by plant-hunters. By contrast, there are also many small, dedicated collections within larger gardens.

Conservation
Many gardens open to the public are active in the areas of conservation and collecting. Look out for national plant collections and seed banks that perform important work conserving, growing, propagating and documenting plant species, as well as making them available to growers.

Specialist houses
In cooler climates citrus fruits are grown in large pots in grand orangeries, which provide them with warmth in winter (in summer they are moved outside). You will also find specialist houses for raising palms, cacti, camellias, orchids and alpines.

Displays
You may find a corner of a garden devoted to an artistic arrangement of one type of plant, such as an auricula theatre. This refers to a display of pots of different varieties of auricula on tiered shelving within a roofed structure designed to keep off the rain.

Plants
If you spot a well-labelled grouping of one type of plant, it may be a dedicated collection. It could variously be a fernery (ferns), a mossery (mosses), a nuttery (nut trees) or even a troughery (plants grown in stone troughs)!

Parks for People

The visual difference between a public park and a private garden is immediately apparent. The former is designed to fulfil the multiple needs of great numbers of urban dwellers. Paths, playing fields, tennis courts, bowling greens, children's play areas, lakes (often with boats for hire), lawns, flower beds, shelters, monuments are all common, while signs, refreshment kiosks and public conveniences are essentials. The scale of such places is often very large but the style of planting and architecture is likely to be far more eclectic than found in a private garden.

Hyde Park, London, England
Public parks provide a vital physical (as well as psychological) space for city and town dwellers. They are an important place of play for adults and children.

N

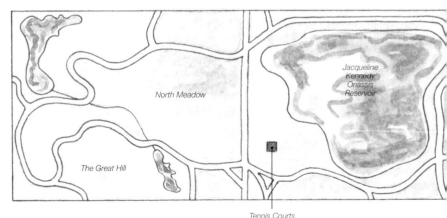

Jacqueline Kennedy Onassis Reservoir

North Meadow

The Great Hill

Tennis Courts

Plan of Central Park, New York, USA
Central Park is the 'green lung' of New York City, an oasis in the Manhattan high-rise landscape. Opened in 1859, it was designed by Frederick Law Olmsted (1822–1903) who had visited many of the new European parks. Particularly influential were two of England's public

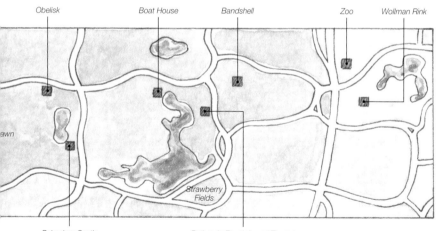

Obelisk   Boat House   Bandshell   Zoo   Wollman Rink

awn

Strawberry Fields

Belvedere Castle   Bethesda Fountain and Terrace

parks: Liverpool's Birkenhead Park and the Derby Arboretum. During the industrial revolution, as towns and cities became increasingly unsanitary and crowded, these parks fulfilled the 19th-century democratic ideal of providing green and healthy open spaces in which citizens could walk, play and take exercise, just as they do today.

Creating a Look

Introduction

A sense of style and place
Look for gardens with a coherent and unified sense of style. The design and planting should unite harmoniously with the surroundings.

A well-developed sense of style is vital to a garden's success. Recognising some of the key elements of historical styles is essential for getting the most from garden visits. Accurately dating a garden can be very difficult; for example, you may not be in an original Dutch baroque garden but a much later one, made 'in the style of …'. However, once you have identified a style you can begin to ask such questions as 'Is this genuine? If not, why was this style chosen? What does it say about the maker?'

Ingredients

Think of the various components of a garden as ingredients, each contributing to the overall style. Manicured lawns and geometric flower borders neatly filled with colourful annual bedding plants are a sure sign of the 19th-century craze for using new strains of plants from around the world.

Function

Do setting, function and style achieve a cohesive whole, or are they at odds with each other? The restrained furniture, containers and planting chosen for this modern terrace are in perfect harmony and stylishly fulfil the purpose for which they were intended.

Plants

Never overlook the basics such as trees, shrubs and flowers when accessing a garden's style. This jumble of summer-flowering country favourites are typical floral ingredients for creating the quintessential cottage garden look.

Eclecticism

Always be prepared for the unexpected in a garden! Not all decorative structures conform to an established style and there is always some room for the innovative and individual. However, too much eclecticism is likely to confuse the viewer.

Gardens of Order

**Chatsworth House,
Derbyshire,
England**
Variations on the
early knot garden
are seen in many
gardens today.
This design is
unusual as it is
raised on a stone
platform.

As any vestiges of early medieval, 14th- and 15th-century gardens have almost certainly been overlaid or obliterated by later designs, the garden visitor is most likely to be enjoying a re-creation or copy. Fortunately, these garden styles survive owing to periodic revivals in their popularity. Such gardens are characterised by a formal symmetry, often of quite elaborate proportions; in grander gardens look for moats, mazes and spiral mounts. Other clues include transitory pleasures such as highly scented flowers and herbs – a necessary choice in less hygienic times!

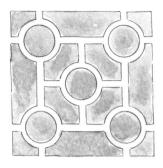

Enclosure

Early privy, or private, gardens were enclosed from the outside world. Close board fences of varying heights were frequently used as these created a solid barrier. Roofed gates formed the entrance to such gardens. Later, hedges or walls replaced the wooden fencing.

Knot gardens

The knot garden is another formal feature, its framework defined by miniature hedges of low-growing evergreen plants such as box with flowers filling the intervening spaces. Early simple chequerboard designs were later superseded by highly complex scrolling patterns.

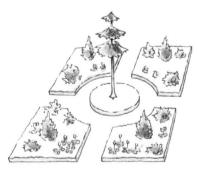

Plants

The Elizabethan aesthetic demanded that individual plants should be spaced evenly apart, allowing full appreciation of the single specimen, rather than the massed effect. The dark expanse of soil between the individual plants acted as a backdrop against which to view the flowers.

Arbours

Several variations of the arbour appear in early formal garden designs, including the tunnel and the covered seat. Simple wooden trellis provides an openwork sheltering wall that also acts as a support for climbing and fragrant plants, bringing their blooms to the level of an appreciative eye and nose.

Gardens of Excess

Italian Renaissance architects designed buildings and gardens based on a revival of the ideals of classical antiquity. Enormous, powerful and elaborate gardens were the result in the late 15th and early 16th century. All-encompassing, they feature terraces, loggias, avenues, walks, fountains, pools, sculpture, labyrinths, grottoes, groves, topiary, flowers, banqueting houses and much else. These villa gardens are symbolic and emblematic, their elements convey a complex visual language of allusion and allegory. In England, Renaissance gardens were theatrical and featured diversions such as masked performances but all were swept away by the landscape movement.

Villa Lante, Bagnaia, Italy
Based on Ovid's *Metamorphoses*, the symbolic scheme of the garden at the 16th-century Villa Lante represents humanity's fall from the Golden Age. Its lavish centrepiece is the Fontana del Quadrato.

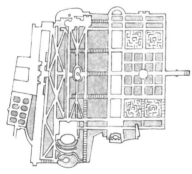

Layout
This plan of the Villa d'Este, Tivoli, Italy, shows the complexity of layout that is so typical of the Italian Renaissance garden. Key features of their design are the strong axes that bisect the garden in various directions and the symmetry of their often highly elaborate parterres.

Water
Sophisticated hydraulic engineering is used to power a fantastic array of water features including fountains, jets, cascades and *giochi d'acqua* (water jokes). Their design is endlessly inventive and many are adorned with sculptural figures that represent river gods and water nymphs.

Sculpture

You will encounter numerous fine sculptural groups strategically placed throughout the Renaissance garden, such as this sculpture of Hercules and Antaeus at the Villa Medici de Castello in Florence, Italy. Many have been copied, their likeness appearing in gardens throughout the world.

Grottoes

Fantastic grottoes were common in grand gardens by the mid-16th century. Based upon the classical Greek notion of the nymphaeum, a place where offerings were made to nymphs, in Renaissance gardens they often have a formal exterior yet inside are more cave-like.

French & Dutch Formality

Het Loo Palace, Apeldoorn, the Netherlands
Often rather misleadingly referred to as the 'Versailles of Holland', Het Loo originally dates from the 1680s. What we visit today is a 1970s restoration and re-creation.

The gardens at the Château de Versailles in France are the epitome of French style and derive directly from Italian Renaissance gardens. Adapted to suit the flatter terrain, the grand design is characterised by great expanses of still water and surface pattern. Parterres are placed close to the house to be viewed from above, long avenues radiate out from the house towards perimeter *bosquets* (shrubberies), intersected by walks. Impressive fountains, sculpture and balustrading abound. Out of the grandiose French style, smaller Dutch gardens developed in the 17th century featuring hedges, topiary, statuary and, of course, canals and tulips.

Planted patterns

The French developed and refined the style of bedding known as the parterre. The most elaborate, *parterres de broderie*, are positioned closest to the house, with simpler designs at a greater distance. These complex arabesque patterns derived from the heavily embroidered clothes of the period. Flowing intricate designs are bordered in low-growing box with flowers and foliage plants grown in the beds. Some compartments are filled with raked coloured materials such as coal dust or sand.

Box Hedging

Box Hedging

Sand/gravel

Clipped Topiary

Box hedging

Sand/gravel

Sand/gravel

Clipped Topiary

Box Hedging

Clipped Topiary

English Landscape

The 18th-century English landscape garden was a reaction against the dominant French and Dutch formality. Influenced by the landscape paintings of Claude and Poussin, celebrated designers like Lancelot 'Capability' Brown (1716–83) turned the grounds of stately homes into idealised views of nature. The archetypal landscape garden is large; it has a vast irregular lake; sweeping lawns right up to the house; trees, singly or in clumps, carefully positioned throughout the garden; and belts of native trees surround the perimeter, beyond which is a boundary drive.

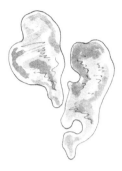

The ha-ha

The antithesis of the enclosed garden, the landscape park dispenses with boundaries so the landscape beyond becomes part of the garden. The ingenious ha-ha is a steep ditch that keeps out grazing animals without the need for intrusive fencing.

Water

You will not find formal geometric pools in these gardens as rivers and streams were dammed and great serpentine lakes cut into the landscape, hence the eponymous Serpentine in Kensington Gardens, London. Occasionally sinuous rills were introduced.

Paths

Straight, axial paths are anathema to the landscape garden; rather paths curve and meander through lawns and trees out to the 'wilderness' beyond. They are designed to lead the visitor to the best positions for viewing and appreciating various composed 'scenes' throughout the garden.

Buildings

Look for carefully sited buildings of Classical design. Most commonly these are small temples and often named after a deity such as Venus. Frequently these buildings are positioned on a slight incline overlooking a lake to create a reflection when viewed from the opposite bank.

Playful Gardens

In France, Germany and England the rococo garden gained popularity towards the end of the 18th century. In a new mood of playfulness, the Picturesque Movement took the visitor on a journey through the garden presenting views, or 'pictures', intended to evoke certain emotional responses. In their more extreme forms these atmospheric landscapes alluded to literary ideas of the Sublime with untamed, rugged and spectacular scenes, often with a precipitous abyss! Incorporating an eclectic mix of styles, they are light-hearted, elegant, feminine and intended for pleasure and entertainment.

Painshill Park, Surrey, England
A perfect example of theatricality and artifice, the fake 'stalactites' that hang from the 18th-century grotto ceiling are made from wooden laths, plaster and chips of calcite, fluorite and gypsum!

Ruins
The irregular, asymmetrical appearance of a ruin seems particularly appropriate in a Picturesque setting. It evokes musings on the passage of time and the impermanence of all things. Always wander behind a ruined building, as many are nothing more than a sham façade!

Hermitages
Often incorporated into these gardens are rustic constructions deemed suitable abodes for Picturesque hermits. These may have housed hired 'hermits' in days gone by, their scurrying bearded figures glimpsed through the trees. A simpler alternative is the small rustic cottage.

Grottoes

More naturalistic than Italian Renaissance grottoes, the rococo grotto was highly decorative, with elaborate rock and shell work and sometimes mirrors. (Rococo originates from the French for rockwork and shell so it is fitting that grottoes are such a feature of these gardens.)

Structures

Lightweight and decorative designs are commonly chosen for rococo garden structures. Gothic seats, Chinese bridges and Turkish tents are all typical. In this context these styles were considered less serious and more playful than their classical counterparts.

Flowering Formality

Tolquhon Castle, Aberdeenshire, Scotland
Gardens of such extreme formality as this demand skill, expertise and continuous maintenance. Even if it is not to everyone's taste, the level of perfection cannot fail to impress.

The Victorian era saw the flower garden firmly back in vogue. 'Bedding out' became the craze in Britain, Germany and the USA: brightly coloured annuals, newly introduced from abroad, were raised in heated greenhouses then planted out in formally arranged beds, the designs changing with the season. These may be familiar to you from their continued use in public parks, often as floral clocks or coats of arms. The Italianate style of architecture dominated the garden, as well as the house, with a return to a greater formality characterised by balustraded terraces, axial paths, fountains and statuary.

Plants

Popular in private gardens and public spaces, carpet bedding is a highly skilled and labour-intensive planting scheme. Great quantities of foliage and flowering plants are planted out in colourful patterns and maintained at a uniform height (hence the term 'carpet').

Glasshouses

By the 19th century greenhouses and conservatories were affordable by the middle classes and no longer relegated to the kitchen garden. Conservatories became an integral part of the house, used for entertaining as well as raising exotics, such as gardenias and orchids.

Decoration

A high level of decoration on planters and garden furniture suggests the Victorian era. Mass-produced cast-iron seating often had elaborate embellishments, and particularly popular were rustic and gothic styles and botanical forms such as this fern bench.

Detail

Note the high level of ornamental detailing throughout these gardens. Paths are kept neat and flowers contained by the use of decorative edging. The ropework pattern, also known as barley twist, can still be found in many gardens.

The Humble Plot

Small in scale and humble in origin, cottage gardens evolved outside the frame of fashion and status yet became an influential and much-emulated style. Created for many centuries by impoverished country dwellers, they are a distinctive mix of aesthetic pleasure and necessity; bountiful spaces where flowers compete with herbs, vegetables and fruit. Championed by the influential garden writers William Robinson (1838–1935) and Gertrude Jekyll (1843–1932), in the 19th century the cottage garden became a much-admired symbol of rural simplicity, in strong contrast to the squalor of urban overcrowding. Its European equivalent is the potager.

The quintessential cottage garden
The most successful cottage gardens appear as if no human hand has shaped them, rather they seem a wonder of serendipitous self-seeding!

Boundaries

High walls and fences are expensive to build and maintain so you are more likely to find cottage gardens enclosed by a low wall (made of local materials), a simple fence or, commonly, a mixed hedge of native plants.

Plants

The cottage garden overflows with plants raised from seed, taken from cuttings, swapped with neighbours or self-sown at will, but rarely bought. These are old-fashioned native varieties, subtle in form and shade, not exotic introductions.

Food

Look for beehives and chicken coops because the true cottage garden is as much larder as garden. Herbs grow in profusion by the back door for ease of harvesting and, as ground space is at a premium, pots accommodate any overflow.

Improvisation

Little is wasted in the cottage garden: materials are recycled for productivity and beauty. You frequently see vegetables grown in old tin containers and reclaimed wood used to construct a rustic arch for supporting a rambling rose or honeysuckle.

The Artist in the Garden

The late-Victorian and Edwardian English Arts and Crafts movement originated with the theories of John Ruskin (1819–1900) and William Morris (1834–96) and in America was developed by architects such as Frank Lloyd Wright (1867–1959). With its free use of local vernacular materials and traditional skills it became an important garden style, chiming closely with Irish horticulturist William Robinson who advocated the 'wild garden'. Gertrude Jekyll was one of its greatest practitioners, producing hundreds of planting plans for British, American and European gardens (although she visited few), all characterised by a harmonious mix of formality and a profusion of plants.

Hidcote Garden, Gloucestershire, England
With its extensive garden rooms, crisp yew hedging and box topiary, Hidcote, created by the American Lawrence Johnston (1871–1958) over a hundred years ago, is a perfect example of the Arts and Crafts gardening ethos.

Buildings
Take note of bespoke and individual garden buildings and see how they relate to the style and fabric of the house, because frequently the same architectural vocabulary is echoed in both. Generous arches, semi-circular steps and buttresses are all Arts and Crafts favourites.

Pergolas
The well-planted pergola is found in many of these gardens. The columns are often constructed of tiered narrow stone slabs or tile ends, with substantial timber beams providing the horizontal support. Pergolas may lead off from the main house or be free-standing.

Furniture

Leading Arts and Crafts architect Edwin Lutyens (1869–1944) designed many British houses and their accompanying gardens. Along with elements such as fountains, paths and pergolas he produced this bench, known as the Thakeham, copies of which are still found in gardens today.

Art pottery

The art of the hand-crafted artefact is celebrated in these gardens. Look for items such as this jardinière. Often mistakenly attributed to Gertrude Jekyll, it was actually designed by Mary Watts (1849–1938) and made by the Compton Potters Art Guild.

Suburban Gardens

Suburban front garden, USA
In contrast to its British counterpart, the classic American suburban front lawn presents an inviting face and sense of space to the world beyond, unencumbered by a forbidding hedge, fence or gate.

In Britain the growth of garden cities and the inter-war building of detached and semi-detached suburban housing created small-scale gardens and a new type of gardener: the enthusiastic amateur. Back and front gardens perform different functions: at the rear is a private space used by all the family, while the front garden is neat and ordered, presenting a tidy face to the world, bordered by a low wall, hedge or fence. By contrast the generous front lawns of American suburbia sweep right down to the pavement without interruption or enclosure, like mini landscape parks, whereas European apartment gardening is characterised by overflowing window boxes.

Suburban back garden plan

Unlike great landed estates, British suburban gardens suffer from regular changes of ownership and successive 'tinkering' with their layouts. However, you are still likely to find vestiges of this classic design in many rear gardens today. The long, narrow shape is typical of such plots and, as here, this is often accentuated by long paths and borders running down each side. A terrace marks the transition from house to garden and the large expanse of lawn ensures the time-honoured Sunday morning mowing regime!

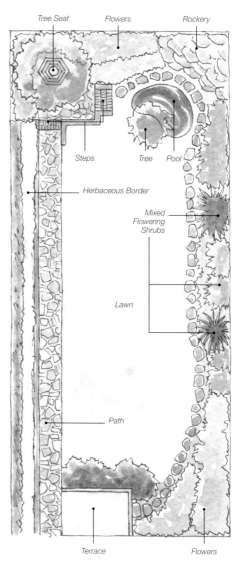

Tree Seat   Flowers   Rockery

Steps   Tree   Pool

Herbaceous Border

Mixed Flowering Shrubs

Lawn

Path

Terrace   Flowers

New Gardens, New World

Safra Bank, São Paulo, Brazil
This roof garden by the great Brazilian landscape gardener and plantsman Roberto Burle Marx (1909–94) is like an abstract painting. Built of stone and gravel, it has minimal planting which can withstand the hot dry conditions.

As in previous centuries, gardens of the 20th century were influenced by new trends in architecture and painting. Modernist architect Le Corbusier (1887–1965) incorporated high-level gardens on the balconies and roofs of his apartment blocks, continuing ancient traditions dating back to the Hanging Gardens of Babylon (*c*.600 BC) and the Aztecs. Large expanses of glass used for walls and windows dissolve the boundaries between garden and interior. Geometrically arranged trees, large open lawns, a preference for evergreens over flowers and still, reflective pools all complement both public and private Modernist buildings.

Materials

Modern gardens use an array of hard materials, often highly coloured. Wood, stone, gravel, steel and glass are common but it is concrete that has freed designers to produce structures such as this curved wall, made from poured and shuttered concrete.

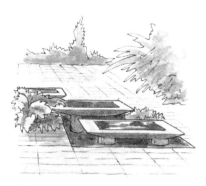

Plants

Plants often appear subservient to structural forms in modern gardens. This tiered container is more about the interplay of horizontal planes and the relationship of one form to another, than about providing a suitable place for things to grow.

Minimalism

Order, restraint and minimal planting make Gabriel Guevrekian's 1925 Cubist Garden at Hyères, France, the model modern garden. Echoes of its style, sadly often debased, can still be seen in gardens today. It is most suited to hot and sunny climes.

Sculpture

Modern gardens provide the perfect visual environment for displaying large sculptural works. You will find long-established dedicated sculpture parks in the United States and in Scandinavia and they are quickly gaining popularity elsewhere. Look for site-specific commissioned pieces.

Gardens Today

It is probably safe to say that at no other time in history have gardens embraced such a diverse range of styles. Certainly, new gardens are still being made on an impressive scale, many utilising advanced developments in technology to create water displays that rival those of the great Italian and French gardens. However, awareness of environmental concerns and our impact on the natural world is now shaping the appearance of our gardens. Look out for the 'prairie' style of garden, characterised by large drifts of late-flowering perennials and grasses which extend the seasonal interest.

Lady Farm, Somerset, England
Unlike traditional herbaceous borders of previous ages, the prairie-like grassland style of planting provides interest across a number of seasons.

Plants
You will notice a renewed interest in native species that are suited to particular climatic conditions as gardeners deal with increasingly unpredictable seasons. Concerns about water shortage and use of limited resources such as peat is also affecting what we plant.

Scale
Gardens that are ambitious in scale and intent are still being made all over the world. Continuing the tradition of making gardens of meaning, a tour of Charles Jencks' Garden of Cosmic Speculation near Dumfries, Scotland, stimulates the visitor visually and intellectually.

Tradition

New and inventive ways have been found of using traditional formal garden elements such as vistas, pools and fountains. At The Alnwick Garden, Northumberland, England, the Grand Cascade is just one of many new ground-breaking water features.

Ornament

The rusting, reclaimed *objets trouvés* used by Derek Jarman (1942–94) to ornament his desolate, shingle beach 'garden' at Dungeness, Kent, England, could not seem more appropriate. Despite many imitations, few have such style and originality.

Introduction

**Parc de Sceaux,
Paris, France**
Consider the
imaginative vision
needed to plant this
splendid avenue of
trees. The original
designer would
never have lived to
see them achieve
this stature.

It is hard to imagine a garden, however small, without
trees. Yet whatever artifice we employ to shape, arrange
and distort living elements in the name of making a
garden, it is the tree that remains most as nature intended.
Their longevity can result in undesirable consequences
such as shade or drainage problems, or damage from roots,
so note the skilful (or otherwise) foresight of the designer.
Be aware of the sizes and locations of existing trees as these
are reliable clues to the age and original layout of a garden.
(You cannot grow a tree quickly!)

Woods

Attached to many large gardens and public parks are woodlands, or even small forests, usually positioned at the periphery. In a woodland, seasonal changes are most noticeable, as is wildlife, the latter far more tolerated than in formal areas of a garden.

Avenues

If you see a straight line of trees you know you are in a man-made environment! Many varieties are used to create long avenues and grand approaches. Although these vistas seem to invite the visitor, they can also be intimidating.

Pruning

Gardeners endeavour to train trees into forms to suit the context and purpose, with the art of bonsai being the most extreme form of 'pruning'. However, left to its own devices, a tree will seek to grow to its natural shape and size.

Function

Trees are one of the most productive plants in the garden. As well as providing wood, many bear fruit or nuts, and are either integrated into the main garden or placed in designated areas such as orchards, kitchen gardens or citrus groves.

Landscaping

Blenheim Palace, Oxfordshire, England

A successful landscape park offers the visitor a series of carefully composed views. Note the balanced composition of lake, trees and architecture.

The visionary 17th- and 18th-century designers who laid out grand and imposing landscapes, such as those at the palaces of Versailles and Blenheim, envisaged scenes they would never live to see, as the trees would take decades to mature and create the desired effects. Often it is today's garden visitor who is enjoying the realisation of these ambitious schemes. If you see a young tree that has replaced one that has died, look at the contrast in scale with those around it for an idea of just how different the immature landscape would have appeared.

Thicket

Note whether trees are planted singly or in groups, close together or more widely spaced. A thicket is a tightly planted group and is sometimes referred to as a wilderness. From a distance it will appear as a dark and heavy shape.

Clump

A clump is a group of trees less densely planted than a thicket. They are a common feature of 'Capability' Brown landscapes; he often placed clumps of beech on the top of hills or on slopes.

Enclosure

Mature trees make an effective screen against sound and wind, as well as providing privacy but, unlike a fence or hedge, they take a long time to establish. A perimeter thick with trees always denotes an old enclosure.

Shrubbery

Shrubberies are usually composed of densely planted woody and flowering shrubs, although some incorporate less vigorous varieties of trees to provide extra height. Often paths are cut through to provide walks, just as in a grove.

Deep in the Woods

Woodlands and forests have been managed and harvested for millennia, and signs of this management are still evident. You often find areas referred to as 'woodland gardens' although these bear little resemblance to a natural native forest or wood. Rather, they are large gardens that have been developed within a more traditional woodland setting and retain a wood-like atmosphere. They are usually created on acid soils with flowering woodland species such as rhododendrons, hydrangeas and magnolias skilfully woven beneath a canopy of taller trees. Bulbous plants carpet the ground in spring.

Bryan Park, Virginia, USA
An understorey of azaleas and redbud trees have been planted to add colour and interest in spring and early summer, before the main forest trees are in full leaf.

Coppice
Coppiced woods have a very particular appearance. Coppicing is a form of medieval management in which trees – especially hazel – are cut back to a stump just above ground level every few years. This causes the tree to sprout many long, slender stems that are useful for firewood, hurdle- and basket-making.

Pollard
A pollard is characterised by its truncated form. Every year the top of the trunk or main branches of a pollard is cut, which encourages multiple stems to grow, well above the height of grazing animals. In winter, look for the great gnarled 'knuckles' at the cut point that give the distinctive silhouette of the pollarded tree.

Belts

Often mistaken for woodland from a distance, a belt is a broad planting of trees, typically around the perimeter of an estate, which creates an effective boundary. Sometimes, on the inner side of a belt, you will also see the drive formerly used by horsedrawn coaches.

Clearing

A clearing in a woodland is known as a 'forest lawn'. It dates back to medieval times when it was used as pasture for the grazing animals of commoners. Within smaller-scale wooded gardens a clearing is sometimes created to introduce an element of surprise.

Garden Groves

Woodland garden
In smaller scale gardens densely planted areas mimic the appearance of a woodland grove. Here a pathway has been cut through to the garden beyond.

A grove, known in Italy as a *bosco*, is a small wood. In Renaissance gardens it is a grove intersected with walks, often planted with evergreens such as holly offering shade and retreat. The French grove is a *bosquet*, a dense planting of trees, or sometimes shrubs, again with walks cut through. An open grove is filled with large, shady trees planted irregularly, while a close grove contains smaller trees underplanted with shrubs to provide some privacy.

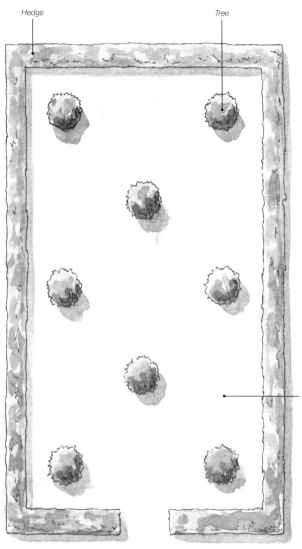

Hedge

Tree

Grass

Quincunx

Look for trees planted in the pattern that indicates 'five' on a die: this is known as a quincunx and can be repeated, as in this plan. Positioned at some distance from the house, such a little wooded arrangement is rather confusingly known as a wilderness, despite being very ornamental rather than 'wild' in appearance. They are usually enclosed from the rest of the garden. You will also notice clipped evergreens planted in the quincunx formation in formal gardens.

Arboreta

Although an arboretum is essentially a large area of ground filled with trees, there is no way you will mistake one for a forest or a wood. Devoted to the collection and display of many species of tree, each specimen is planted so the viewer can appreciate its size and form without competition from its neighbours. Trees may be arranged thematically, most commonly by provenance, or perhaps for their seasonal interest such as spectacular autumn colour. If you find an arboretum within a larger garden, it often reflects an individual's passion for collecting.

Space

A sense of space and openness is one of the chief characteristics of an arboretum, and is quite unlike an enclosed wood. The form of great specimen trees can be appreciated from a distance and even groups are planted with plenty of room in between.

Identification

Trees are almost always well labelled with their name and their country of origin. Some arboreta also provide printed maps or trails so the visitor can wander through the collection and read information about each type of tree.

Seating

Do take advantage of strategically positioned seats when wandering around an arboretum or garden. Following in the landscape tradition, these will have been specially placed to give you the very best view of your surroundings.

Seasonal interest

Arboreta certainly repay repeat visits as they offer very different rewards in different seasons. Many have highly specialised collections of bulbs that carpet the ground in spring while deciduous trees will steal the show in autumn.

A Walk Down the Avenue

An avenue is a long, straight walk or drive lined with evenly placed trees or hedges. An alley, or what in French is known as an *allée*, is the same but tends to be less broad. (This term can also mean a long, narrow lawn used for ball games.) Avenues were employed by designers in the Italian Renaissance to unify and connect disparate parts of a garden, each terminating in a strong focal point such as a building or large sculpture. You will see grand avenues in many French, Dutch, British and American gardens.

Packwood House, Warwickshire, England
This avenue of regularly spaced columns of clipped yew lends an air of solemnity and gravitas to the long approach to the house.

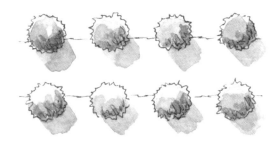

Informal avenue
In more informal gardens you may find an avenue or alley planted in a diagonal formation that creates a less rigid and more relaxed effect. This is often chosen if an avenue has been created in a wood.

Formal avenue
The formal avenue is laid out to a strict geometric grid with trees planted at precise and regular distances from each other. The scale and simplicity of this design creates a powerful effect and imparts to the visitor a sense of arrival.

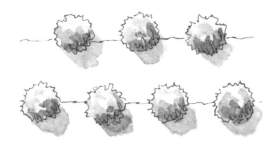

Multiple rows

In gardens of great scale and wealth more than one row of trees, or a mixture of trees and hedging, may be found. Planted in descending order of height, note how secondary alleys are created in between the rows.

Patched avenues

Few avenues of great age retain all their original trees. Diseased and dying specimens need to be replaced by young trees, which is known as patching. The problem can be further compounded as the exact variety may no longer be available.

The Long View

RHS Chelsea Flower Show, London, England
In 2009 the Champagne Laurent Perrier Garden used a simple avenue of pleached hornbeams to create a strong design statement and to direct the gaze to a sculpture.

To create a vista the garden maker must channel the viewer's attention in a chosen direction. Distance is the key to achieving dramatic and awe-inspiring vistas, such as the grand avenues that feature in large-scale gardens. However, good effects can also be achieved in more intimate spaces, and many contemporary designers subvert the idea of the 'long view' by introducing short, tightly constructed vistas in relatively small areas. Whatever the scale, look for vistas that are focused on a single object, such as a scene, building, an obelisk or a simple flower-filled urn.

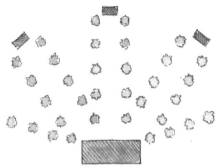

Perspective

Look carefully for a vista that has been deliberately exaggerated by manipulation. Instead of a row of trees planted in parallel lines, they will converge slightly at one end and also descend in height, increasing the visual sense of recession.

Multiple vistas

In very formal gardens you may find a feature known in French as a *patte d'oie*, or goose's foot. Alleys radiate out in a fan shape like the toes of a goose, often from a building, each one terminating in a different feature.

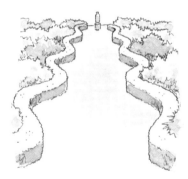

Informality

Vistas are also important and effective design devices in small informal gardens. A simple willow arch festooned with sweet peas creates a fragrant tunnel that gives the garden a sense of structure and order it might otherwise lack.

Height

Tall trees or hedges are not the only means by which to create a vista. Low planting can also direct the eye in a specific direction. Even a simple path across a lawn can lead the gaze towards the desired object.

Stumperies

Magic Garden, Hampton Court, England

This garden for the 2008 Flower Show contrasts the airy lightness and delicacy of the wild flowers against the backdrop of the rather gloomy and gothic stumpery.

The unexpected is often lurking in some dark and dank corner of a garden waiting to take the unsuspecting visitor by surprise, but perhaps few are as unexpected as the stumpery. A stumpery consists of old uprooted tree stumps that have been set upside down into earth banks to reveal all the gnarled complexities of the root structure. The first stumperies were invented by Victorian gardeners and, while not common, they have enjoyed something of a revival in recent years with new ones being introduced into corners of large and small gardens.

Stumps

Large-scale stumperies use the roots of very old trees that require heavy machinery to haul them into place. These great natural sculptures are best suited to dark and damp areas where they impart an air of mystery and a slight gothic menace.

Plants

Often, smaller-scale single stumps are placed among collections of ferns in older gardens (during the Victorian era there was a craze for growing these plants). They provide the perfect growing environment for ferns, ivies, mosses and lichens.

Wildlife

In particularly ambitious stumperies you will find improvised architectural structures such as arches and steep banks that have been formed from giant stumps. As well as being highly atmospheric, they are havens for birds, small mammals and insects.

Ornament

Stumps can be used as decorative features in a garden and associate especially well with rustic ornament as both allude to woodlands and forests. This strange construction forms a kind of bower with a simple seat within.

Fruit & Formality

Fruit trees in commercial orchards are usually planted in straight rows to make harvesting more efficient, whereas those found in gardens are likely to be much smaller in extent and less formally arranged. Look for hives (bees are important for pollination), free-ranging hens and even pigs snuffling about under the trees in autumn. In kitchen gardens there is a tradition of severely pruning and training fruit trees into geometric shapes to restrict their size, improve fruiting and make harvesting easier. Such a tree is known as an espalier.

Espaliered fruit tree
Spring blossom adorns this old espaliered apple, promising a bumper crop in autumn.

Horizontal T
You often see a row of free-standing trees trained in this horizontal design and used as a hedge to line a path. Initially the branches are supported on rods or strong wire frames that are removed once the shape is established.

Palmette verrier
Espaliers are also trained against walls or fences, especially in old walled kitchen gardens. Apart from providing support, this method has the added benefit of the warmth and shelter of the wall, perfect for ripening fruit.

Palmette oblique

A wide variety of fruit trees can be pruned into an espalier including apple, pear, nectarine, peach and apricot. Lower-growing varieties, however, tend to respond best to this treatment. Look out for espaliers of great age and character.

Belgian fence

The technique of espaliering and pleaching is akin to topiary as the end result is highly decorative and ornamental. This intricate pattern, known as the Belgian fence, is especially complex and takes a high degree of skill (and patience) to achieve.

Trees in the Air

A pleached tree is the antithesis of a tree found in a natural woodland. It is one of the most severe examples of the gardener shaping growing plants into architectural forms. Often referred to as a pole hedge, a straight row of pleached trees is literally a 'hedge on stilts'. It can be used in a garden to divide up space while keeping an air of openness and space. Commonly used varieties of trees are elm, lime, hornbeam and beech, the last looking especially good over the winter months.

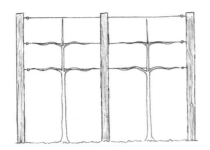

Method

Successful pleaching relies on precise measurement. Regularly spaced stakes support strong wires attached horizontally. Young trees are planted in between and lateral branches trained along the wires. The outward-facing branches are cut off.

Result

Once the trees have matured the stakes are removed, although the wires may be left in place for support. The branches are intertwined in such a way that at canopy level it is impossible to differentiate the individual trees.

Geometry

Although a very old technique, you will frequently see pleaching used by contemporary designers as it is so perfectly suited to creating strong geometric forms. Low, clipped evergreens are often grown at ground level as a visual counterbalance.

Space

Space can be at a premium in modern gardens. The size and shape of a pleached tree is rigorously controlled and contained. This means it is also a very good way to utilise height in the garden without creating too much shade.

Putting on a Show

Introduction

**Glorious tulips
provide colour
in springtime**
While a garden's
evergreen structure
changes little
throughout the year,
flowers provide a
kaleidoscope of
seasonal colour,
form and scent.

If foliage plants are the building blocks of the garden, flowers are the ephemeral stars. The beauty of a flowering garden can be breathtaking but look closely to see just how this has been achieved. Are the chosen plants suited to climate and conditions, do they thrive or struggle? Is this a plant expert's garden, full of excellent or unusual varieties (and occasionally has their selection been to the detriment of aesthetic effects)? Or do you find yourself in an artist's garden with the emphasis on colour and form, rather than horticultural know-how?

Colour

Always be aware of colour in the garden. Does this gardener favour subtle shades or primary colours? Do flowers complement each other or clash? Has a designer deliberately restricted his or her palette of colours and, if so, to what effect?

Scent

Scent is often neglected when planning a garden yet perfume is one of the chief pleasures a plant can offer. Apart from the obvious delights of flowers such as the rose, honeysuckle or nicotiana, many plants – especially herbs – have aromatic leaves.

Ornament

Annuals – plants that are sown, flower and die within a year – are primarily grown for their highly prized ornamental qualities. Their glory is often spectacular but fleeting and contributes nothing to the long-term structure of a garden.

Function

Functional plants, such as fruit, herbs and vegetables, are often very attractive in their own right as well as being edible. Look carefully at a garden that combines flowers and vegetables as it is not solely about food production, but also about beauty.

Floral Carpets

A flower bed is any collection of flowering plants, either massed together or arranged into patterns. The 19th-century craze for carpet bedding echoed the tradition of knot gardens and parterres and, after the austerity of the landscape garden, brought flowers close to the house again. The art of carpet bedding is all about manipulation and control, and early purists used only foliage, removing buds before they could flower. However, the lure of newly introduced garish flowers proved too great, and soon fanciful beds of the brightest colours were seen everywhere.

Carpet bed
If you are lucky enough to see a fine example of the art of carpet bedding, take careful note of the skill and attention to detail deployed.

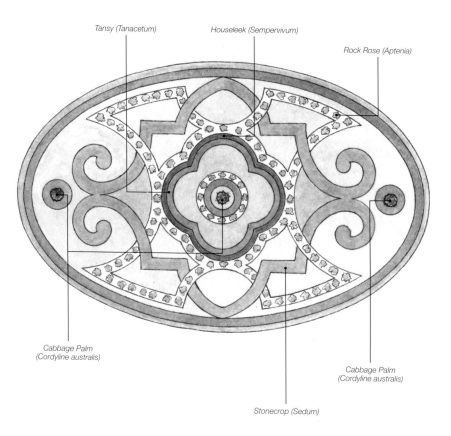

Tansy (Tanacetum)

Houseleek (Sempervivum)

Rock Rose (Aptenia)

Cabbage Palm
(Cordyline australis)

Cabbage Palm
(Cordyline australis)

Stonecrop (Sedum)

Carpet bed design

Circular or oval shapes are more common than linear geometric beds, sometimes rising to a mound in the centre to display the design better. You may see a civic insignia or emblem depicted in municipal parks and gardens. The design is picked out in one main type of plant with another used for edging, and what is known as a 'dot' plant (often spiky, like a palm) to add height. The pattern is then infilled with a changing array of plants such as bulbs, succulents and annuals.

Ribbons & Islands

The Dell Garden, Norfolk, England
Here a number of well-planted island beds are interspersed between mature specimen trees. The arrangement creates a coherent and connected design.

Ribbon beds were popular in the USA and Britain in the 19th century. They are long narrow borders with continuous strips, of equal width, composed of brightly coloured low-growing plants. The beds may be straight, often edging either side of a path, or shaped and cut into a lawn. Island beds are rather more naturalistic. Usually circular or kidney-shaped, they are cut into lawns and planted with mixed shrubs, flowers and often a small tree. Unlike a conventional bed set against a wall or hedge, island beds allow the plants to be viewed from all angles.

Ribbon bed

Garish ribbon beds fell out of fashion by *c.*1900 and are now rare. You may occasionally encounter them flanking the edge of a path in a public garden. They should be very low, the plants either neatly trimmed or pegged close to the ground.

Ribbon designs

Scrolls and repeat motifs were also popular ribbon designs. At their height of popularity this style of planting was used to edge shrubberies (often with a thin row of tiles between the bed and the lawn) and even spread to schemes for containers.

Island bed

The scale of island beds varies, but the most visually successful is a grouping of several together in a large area. In small gardens they need to be carefully positioned so that they do not appear isolated from the rest of the planting.

Island designs

Kidney-, or tear-shaped island beds are common. The inclusion of tall shrubs or a tree is useful for screening out unwanted views. Such beds are often used for planting schemes based on a theme, such as exotics or autumn colour.

Brilliant Borders

The herbaceous or perennial border is a deep bed set against a wall or hedge. It can vary in length substantially and may be single, or double – with a path in between. Because of their perennial nature (the plants die back in winter), you may find them sited where they cannot be seen from the house. At the height of summer the success of the herbaceous border rests on a carefully orchestrated balance of colour, volume, height and leaf shape with no soil visible (annuals are used to fill any gaps, along with tender potted plants).

Bois des Moutiers, Varengeville-sur-Mer, France
Gertrude Jekyll used clipped yew to create a series of architectural buttresses along the length of this border to add both rhythm and form.

1 Yucca
2 Crambe maritima
3 Blue Hydrangea
4 White Snapdragon
5 Santolina
6 Yellow Hollyhock
7 White and Yellow Foxgloves
8 Echinops ritro
9 White Dahlia
10 Clematis jackmanii
11 Achillea eupatorium
12 Yellow Snapdragon
13 Cineraria maritima
14 Dictamrius
15 Geranium ibericum
16 Aster acris
17 Aster shortii
18 Verbascum olympicum
19 Aster umbellatus
20 Yew (Taxus) hedge

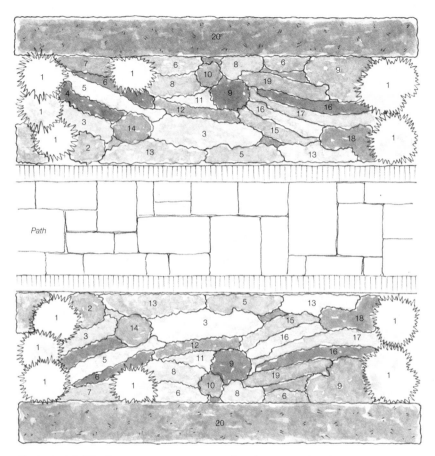

Gertrude Jekyll herbaceous border

From the late 19th century onwards Jekyll took the herbaceous border to new levels of perfection. Skilfully employing a painterly and impressionistic palette of colours, her borders were both subtle and arresting. This small section of one of Jekyll's many plans ranges in colour (beginning on the left) from cream, pink and silver blue, through to pink, pale yellow, white, pale blue, then terminates in blue, white, silver and cream. Spiky yuccas add dramatic structure and a dark yew hedge provides a contrasting background.

Romantic Roses

Roses are one of the oldest known garden flowers. First cultivated by gardeners in Ancient China, they were popular with the Romans and have been prized the world over ever since. As a species they are much hybridised and you will encounter an astonishing range of colours, forms and, most importantly, scents. It is thought that the first garden dedicated solely to the rose was that of the Empress Josephine at the Château de Malmaison, near Paris, in the early 19th century. The vogue quickly spread through France, then to Britain and beyond.

Adelaide Botanic Gardens, South Australia
Built to celebrate Australia's Bicentenary (1988), the Bicentennial Conservatory houses lowland tropical plants, in contrast to the brilliant, but ephemeral roses in the gardens outside.

Weeping standards
Roses are grown formally and informally. In France there is a tradition of using tightly pruned standards, either clipped into balls or as more natural weeping forms. Still popular, these standards feature in many formal gardens today.

Shrubs
Shrub roses are the easiest to manage in a garden. Most modern hybrids repeat flower and have good disease resistance. Old varieties, such as the Gallicas, Centifolias and Damasks, have the shortest flowering times but the best colour and perfume.

Climbers

Climbing roses bring an unmistakable air of romance and glamour to any garden, adding height, colour and fragrance. Most commonly you will see them trained against walls, over arches, entwined in bowers or framing a cottage doorway.

Ramblers

Rambling roses are vigorous and quick-growing varieties that require plenty of space to spread. They are most appropriate growing in more naturalistic settings and happily twine through trees and shrubs, or scramble along banks.

Rose Gardens

Mottisfont Abbey, Hampshire, England
Mottisfont is home to the National Collection of old roses. The structure and formality of the box hedging and timber arches lend form to its walled garden, even when the roses have ceased to flower.

Rose gardens, also known as rosariums or rosaries, are almost always formal. Where space is no problem, you frequently find them sited away from the house and enclosed by walls or hedges. As roses flower for a relatively short period, much of the year these gardens remain unvisited. To suit more modest gardens, influential figures such as Gertrude Jekyll and Vita Sackville-West (1892–1962) began to integrate roses into mixed schemes with other flowering plants, thus extending the overall flowering season. This became the matrix for growing roses you now see throughout the world.

Arches

Look out for traditional ways of supporting roses as these tried-and-tested methods persist in different contexts. Climbers trained around single or multiple arches are frequently used for framing vistas and for lining pathways.

Festoons

Also known as catenaries or swags, this method involves tall posts placed in the ground with thick rope or chains slung between. Roses are grown against the poles and trained down and along the rope or chain, which encourages flowering.

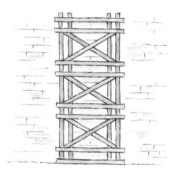

Flat trellis

Climbing roses can easily be trained against a trellis by tying in soft sappy stems. Using flat trellis also screens unsightly walls or fences and, if decorative itself, remains attractive once the rose has lost its leaves and flowers.

Trellis structures

Substantial free-standing trellis supports are perfect for vigorous climbing species. Often found in large formal rose gardens, trellis structures are particularly suited to grand and elegant schemes and add structure in winter.

Knot Gardens

**Bourton House,
Gloucestershire,
England**
In this variation
on an open knot
design, clipped box
trees fill some of the
shapes and add
vertical interest.
The knot design
incorporates a raised
pond at its centre.

From the early 15th century onwards the term parterre (from the Latin *per terre*, on the ground) was used for certain types of decorative beds. Geometric in layout – often square – they developed from the simple four-part plan of Persian gardens. The design can be simple or complex; each quarter may be symmetrical or contain figurative designs such as an heraldic emblem. Parterres, known in England as knot gardens, are formed from low-growing clipped hedges, usually of box, germander or cotton lavender, and are intended to be viewed from above.

Simple knot

Simple knots are formed from one variety of plant. The use of evergreens means that the beds look good throughout the year and you frequently find them positioned in a highly visible place, such as at the entrance to a garden.

Complex knots

Very subtle effects can be achieved by using plants with foliage of varying shades of green, commonly box, lavender, rosemary and rue. If cleverly clipped, the plants appear to twist and curl around each other, as with a true knot.

Open knots

In what is known as an open knot, the design is picked out in a low-growing evergreen and the shapes filled with different coloured materials. Traditionally chalk, coal and brick dust were used but you may see coloured gravel today.

Closed knots

In a closed knot the spaces of the design are densely planted with different flowers. These may be changed throughout the seasons, for instance spring bulbs will be followed by brightly coloured annuals, then left bare in winter.

Parterres

**Pitmedden Garden,
Aberdeenshire,
Scotland**
This parterre
incorporates both
open and closed
compartments, the
latter filled with
flowers that are
changed seasonally.
Pitmedden's six
parterres incorporate
five miles of clipped
box hedge.

Using the same palette of materials as knot gardens, the parterres of the great Italian Renaissance gardens are more ambitious in scale and complex in design than their English counterparts. In the 17th and 18th centuries the French developed and refined the practice, creating a whole vocabulary to distinguish different styles. *Parterres de compartiment* are symmetrical both horizontally and vertically. The *parterre de broderie* is based on the elaborate designs for the heavily embroidered clothing of the period, while there is even the *parterre d'eau*, made with pools of water.

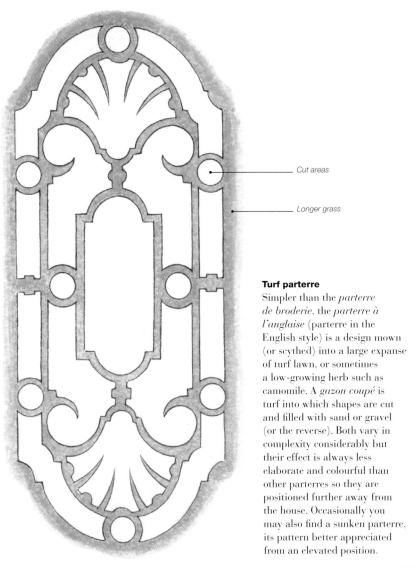

Cut areas

Longer grass

Turf parterre

Simpler than the *parterre de broderie*, the *parterre à l'anglaise* (parterre in the English style) is a design mown (or scythed) into a large expanse of turf lawn, or sometimes a low-growing herb such as camomile. A *gazon coupé* is turf into which shapes are cut and filled with sand or gravel (or the reverse). Both vary in complexity considerably but their effect is always less elaborate and colourful than other parterres so they are positioned further away from the house. Occasionally you may also find a sunken parterre, its pattern better appreciated from an elevated position.

Herb Gardens

Gardens devoted to herbs have a long history: these aromatic plants are some of the earliest cultivated by gardeners, prized for their medicinal, culinary or domestic uses. However, unless you are in one of the great physic gardens of the world, the majority of herb gardens visited today are either copies or modern interpretations of traditional designs. Whether grown formally in a knot pattern, or integrated more naturalistically into a mixed border, the subtle colouring and fragrance of herbs imparts a sense of historical romance and nostalgia unmatched by other groups of plants.

Mature herb garden
The relaxed growing habits of many herbs seem better suited to less formal, more relaxed layouts, such as in this well-established herb garden of a former priory.

Paths
Herbs can be grown in pockets between brick or stone paving. This is especially suitable for ground-hugging varieties such as creeping thyme and camomile. Look for paths that have been created in this way.

Patterns
Herbs look good arranged in a wheel pattern, again using paving to delineate the shape. Height can be added by placing a central feature such as a sundial or tall pot at the centre of the 'spokes'.

Gravel

Many herbs originate from hot, arid Mediterranean regions and thrive in dry, well-drained conditions. Gravel provides the perfect growing medium. You will often see them informally planted in this way in circular arrangements.

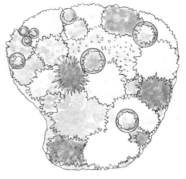

Beds

Rather than a sizeable area, a garden may have just a single bed (often raised) devoted to herbs. Sometimes they are set within a lawn, like island beds, and if planted with low-growing herbs they resemble rich tapestries.

Bog Gardens

Exploiting a watercourse
Lucky is the gardener who has a natural watercourse running through his or her garden. Those less fortunate often create boggy areas at the side of larger ponds.

Bog gardens have an air of mystery, quite unlike the open fountains and pools found in ornamental water gardens. The term 'bog' properly refers to the soft, marshy ground found at the margins of ponds, where run off and organic matter meet, creating a nutrient-rich, swampy environment sought by many moisture-loving plants, as well as by a host of wildlife. Some of the best examples of these gardens have been created by exploiting the margins of shallow streams that meander through light woodland, offering the contrast of running and standing water.

Marginals

Plants that favour the waterlogged soil found at the edges of ponds are known as marginals. They include some of the most attractive spring and summer flowers such as flags, marsh marigold, mimulus and, despite its name, the skunk cabbage.

Accent plants

True pond plants cannot cope with the nutrient-rich environment at the margins of pools and streams. However, luxuriant growth at the water's edge is provided by species that thrive in these conditions, often furnishing a colourful accent.

Scale

The sight of a towering gunnera plant, or its smaller cousin the rheum, is a sure sign of a successful bog garden. Given the right conditions these plants can grow to over head height, earning their common name of 'giant rhubarb'.

Foliage

Although accented by many flowering plants, bog gardens are really all about dramatic foliage. Various forms, sizes and colours of leaf grow deeply layered one against another creating rich contrasts of light and shade.

Sweet Scented Gardens

Gardens intended primarily to stimulate senses other than sight are variously known as scented, sensory or aromatic gardens. Physical signs of such gardens may include guide rails, Braille notices, touch-friendly sculpture, musical wind chimes, yet their most important element remains ephemeral: smell. Flowers selected for a scented garden are chosen for their fragrance above all else, rather than for colour or form, so you are more likely to find older, more subtle varieties than modern hybrids. These have the added benefit of attracting birds and insects too, so remember to listen as well as inhale!

A place to sit amid fragrant beds
During summer seats should be positioned to take full advantage of a garden's perfume, as well as its visual pleasure. The scent of lavender is particularly calming, and will encourage you to linger.

Position
To enjoy their full effect, perfumed flowers need to be on a level with our noses. Planting highly fragrant climbers such as roses, jasmine and honeysuckle around arches, doorways or pergolas not only makes them easy to smell but also maximises wind-borne scent.

Raised beds
Many plants emit wonderful fragrances when their foliage is lightly bruised. Plants such as sage, lavender or scented geraniums overflowing from waist-high raised beds or containers encourage the visitor to brush the leaves gently between their fingers, releasing wonderful aromas.

Paths

Paths lined with guide rails, combined with fragrantly planted raised beds, characterise many gardens specially created for the blind or partially sighted. These gardens originally date from the late 1930s and are now a feature of public parks in many countries.

Seats

Sunny seats surrounded by sweet-smelling plants make the perfect spot to sit and catch their various scents drifting on the wind. At such close proximity the soothing sound of the flutter and hum of myriads of flying insects also ensures auditory as well as olfactory pleasure!

Travelling Plants

Abbey Gardens, Tresco, Isles of Scilly, England
The mild and balmy climate enjoyed by the Isles of Scilly off Cornwall's coast allows many tender exotics to thrive, whereas on the mainland they would struggle to survive.

An 'exotic' is any plant found growing outside its natural habitat. For centuries gardeners the world over have attempted to push the boundaries of what and where they can grow non-native varieties. The trend is as popular as ever, and within many large gardens you find exotic, subtropical or Mediterranean areas. Climate changes in many regions mean that plants once regarded as tender now survive milder winters. Concern about water use has encouraged experiments with 'dry' gardens in which drought-tolerant plants are grown in gravel and only ever watered by rainfall.

Exotic plants

You will recognise these gardens by what you find growing there, rather than by architectural or ornamental features. The layout may be formal or informal but it is always the plants that set the tone and texture of the place.

Season

Exotic planting is best seen in sunshine as this intensifies the vibrancy of flower and foliage colour. In cooler climes such gardens reach their zenith in late summer and early autumn: to enjoy them at their best plan your visit accordingly.

Flowers

Look out for flowers with vibrant colour, such as dahlias and cannas. A jungle-like atmosphere is provided by tall architectural foliage such as that of bamboo, fatsia, pampas grass, banana, agave, yucca and, of course, the ubiquitous palm.

Origin

A successful exotic garden needs a sense of cohesion, a good example of which is The Eden Project, Cornwall, England, where several giant biomes display the plants adapted to very specific conditions, such as those found in tropical rainforests and the drought-prone Mediterranean.

Beautifully Productive

Potager is the French term for an ornamental vegetable or kitchen garden. Equal attention is paid to the aesthetics of this garden as to its produce. Although you will see the same plants here as in other vegetable gardens, they are arranged with far more artistry. Ordered rows of onions and cabbages sit alongside decorative flowers, while low box hedges contain sprawling courgettes or nasturtiums, and topiary shapes punctuate the centres of beds. Plants are grown closer together than in conventional vegetable plots, and there is usually a focal point, perhaps a fruiting arch or walkway.

Artistic and edible
Aesthetics and order dictate the arrangement of this potager, taking precedence over the desire for bumper harvests.

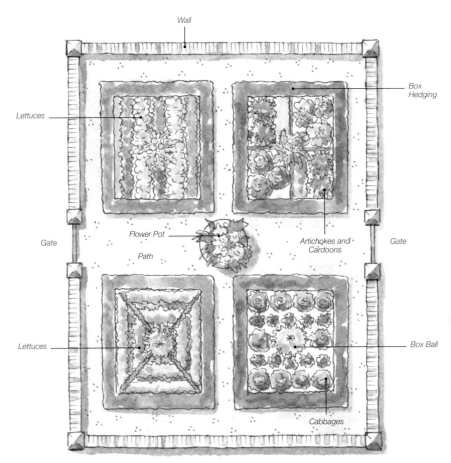

Wall

Box Hedging

Lettuces

Flower Pot

Artichokes and Cardoons

Gate

Gate

Path

Lettuces

Box Ball

Cabbages

The potager

Potagers are tightly filled with a mixture of ornamental vegetables, herbs, fruit and flowers (often edible) arranged in geometric patterns. The stately globe artichoke and spiky cardoon have large, deep-cut silvery green leaves and large round heads, while leafy lettuces offer a pleasing palette from palest green to deepest purple with smooth or frilled textures. Paths, box hedges and pots accent the design while vertical interest is provided by canes supporting climbing annuals such as beans, or sturdy frames bearing pumpkins and squashes.

Edible Gardens

After several decades of sad neglect, many walled kitchen gardens have been restored over recent years. However beautifully tended, these spaces retain an air of functionality. A brief list of just some of the things you may find here gives an idea of what busy places these formerly were. Look for hothouses and hot beds (for raising tender fruit and vegetables), mushroom beds, cold frames (for hardening off seedlings before planting out), vine houses, pineries (for pineapples), forcing pits (for forcing all types of fruit including melons, rhubarb and strawberries) and, most importantly, compost heaps.

The kitchen garden
This paved path is just wide enough for wheelbarrow access and the plant supports are strong and sturdy, rather than decorative. Both are signs of functionality.

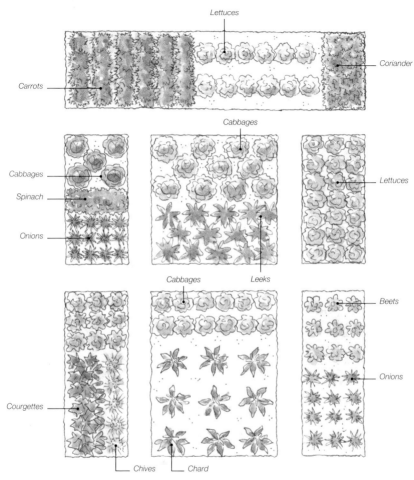

Lettuces

Coriander

Carrots

Cabbages

Cabbages

Spinach

Onions

Lettuces

Cabbages

Leeks

Courgettes

Chives

Chard

Cabbages

Beets

Onions

Vegetable plot

The typical vegetable plot is a series of rectangular beds, either at ground level or raised, arranged around paths to provide access for tending. The beds are compartmentalised so that crops can be grown using the rotation system.

Groups of plants are moved from bed to bed each year to discourage disease. Often the only flowers are 'useful' ones, say those of herbs like chives, or plants such as marigold and hyssop, which may be beneficial in warding off predatory insects. This is known as companion planting.

Kitchen Garden Paraphernalia

For hundreds of years productive vegetable and fruit gardens were as much a feature of grand estates as of humble cottages: only the scale and varieties grown varied. Following wartime campaigns, such as 'Dig For Victory' in Britain and the Victory Gardens in the USA, after the Second World War domestic food-growing gradually fell from favour. However, among many young gardeners growing food is currently enjoying a revival in popularity. A visit to a well-run kitchen garden is inspiring and instructive, as well as offering intriguing insights into the cultivation methods, techniques and tools of the past.

Forcing pots
Many utilitarian objects, such as these forcers, are beautiful as well as functional, and many fragile originals are now collectors' items.

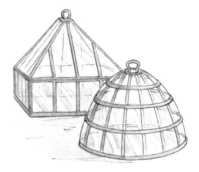

Bell-jars
The large kitchen gardens of the 18th and 19th centuries employed many staff to lavish great attention on their precious crops. To protect individual plants from frost and rain, thick glass bell-jars were used. You may see a few surviving originals.

Hand-lights
A more sophisticated development was the hand-light in which the glass was set into iron frames. Think of these as small greenhouses that fitted over plants for protection. Little doors could be opened to allow for better ventilation.

Forcers

Still available today, rhubarb and sea-kale forcers are large terracotta pots that are placed over young plants. Obscuring the daylight literally 'forces' the plants to strain upwards, producing the desired long pale stems. Small lids allow for inspection.

Water barrow

Before the days of hoses and irrigation systems, water was transported around the garden in water barrows or carts. In a well-appointed kitchen garden you may see the remains of a dipping pool from which water was drawn.

Shaping Nature

Introduction

Gardens are all about artifice. Large or small, ambitious or modest, in some way or other they express a desire to remap the physical world. When you next find yourself in a garden, take a more searching look. Has this landscape been radically remodelled? Is there now a perfectly formed hill where none was before? How does this rolling lawn become, apparently seamlessly, pasture for sheep? Was a stream dammed and diverted to create this extravagantly sinuous lake? Many garden makers seek only to enhance what nature has provided but don't assume this is so; some gardens are wholly the product of human endeavour.

Enhancing nature
In a garden in which such obvious care has been taken in the positioning of features, it is highly unlikely that the gentle rise in the ground has occurred naturally.

Terrain

Never overlook the obvious! Whether manicured lawn, rough pasture or flower-filled meadow, the appearance of the ground beneath your feet is likely to be the result of manmade decisions, choices and maintenance regimes, not serendipity.

Topography

Throughout history garden makers have gone to great lengths to remodel their landscapes (and many still do). Take note whether the finished result appears wholly natural or deliberately artificial and ask why this might have been the desired effect.

Water

Ever since gardens began to be made, water has been a highly prized component. Any garden that includes a naturally occurring lake or stream within its boundaries offers a marvellous advantage. Manipulation of water is difficult and costly.

Ornament

In addition to remodelling a landscape, garden makers frequently use living elements such as plants and water as ornamental and decorative features. The effects are various, from adding an air of grandeur to a sense of playfulness.

The Green Grass of 'Home'

The term 'lawn' can refer to the sweeping expanse of rolling grassland typical of the landscape park, or a handkerchief-sized patch outside a domestic dwelling. In each case the cool, green stretch of grass acts as a visual resting place between architectural features, busy borders or vertical hedges. Prior to the widespread introduction of mechanised grass cutting, vast lawns were a sign of wealth, demonstrating the economic ability to control untidy nature with small armies of scythe-wielding gardeners. Even today, lawn maintenance to a high standard is both costly and time consuming.

Providing a route
Visitor traffic through a garden can be gently guided by closely mown paths, providing routes through an otherwise random landscape.

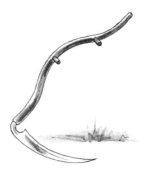

Scythe

Unless grazed by animals, the highly efficient tool known as a scythe was used to cut lawns from Roman times until the 19th century. This skilled task produced excellent results and involved teams of men arranged in slow-moving rows.

Mower

Grass cutting was revolutionised by the invention of the mechanical mower in 1830. Early models were horsedrawn (the animals clad in leather 'boots' to protect the lawn) or hand-pushed and later superseded by steam-powered and petrol versions.

Roller

The perfect lawn must be flat and smooth. To this end heavy garden rollers are used to make and maintain lawns. Originally of stone or wood, iron rollers became popular in the 19th century and were widely used to produce a sward unspoilt by bumps.

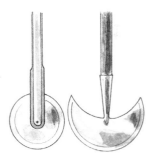

Edging tools

The smooth, green sward was complemented by crisp sharp edges of beds and borders, and paths free from lateral shoots. Modern gardeners still use traditional tools such as the circular wheel and half-moon cutter blades to achieve this look.

Flowery Meads & Meadows

Before mechanical cutting and chemical weed-control, lawns more closely resembled what today we think of as a wildflower meadow. Intermingled with grasses grew a range of flowering plants, including camomile, thyme, ox-eye daisy, periwinkle and clover. Traditional meadows are under threat from changing agricultural practices and sadly many ancient examples have been lost. In recent decades some gardeners have sought to redress the balance by establishing flowering meadow areas within a more traditional garden setting.

Midsummer meadow
Although large meadows in rural settings look quite wonderful, smaller scale areas (such as verges) can also be very effective when carefully managed to encourage wild flowers.

Seasons
Unlike lawns, which are intended to be a uniform green throughout the year, the appearance of meadows varies seasonally. A meadow in late winter may just look like a field, whereas in spring or late summer it can be a mass of colour and scent.

Management
Successful meadows need careful managing that involves the cutting and removal of grass at certain times of the year, once plants have flowered and set seed. Wildflowers thrive in poor soil so nutrient-rich cuttings should not be left to rot down.

Mown paths

A mown path meandering through long grass repays investigation. Often found at the periphery of a garden, this can indicate that a meadow area is being established. Old orchards make suitable sites as they have usually seen less chemical treatment.

Wildlife

As the complete antithesis of chemically maintained lawns, meadows provide vital habitats for all kinds of wildlife. Sit quietly among the flowers and listen to the hum and buzz of literally thousands of insects and birds busying themselves around you.

Garden Games

Kingston Maurward Gardens, Dorset, England

In grand formal gardens, with dedicated 'rooms' or compartments, you often find a games lawn. When there is no play, these green swards offer an oasis of calm.

Areas within gardens dedicated to the playing of lawn games have been common since the medieval period. A flat expanse of tightly mown grass may suggest to you a lawn used for croquet or bowling (a gradual rise towards the centre of the green denotes the more complex game of crown green, rather than flat green, bowling). Lawn tennis courts are often hidden from view behind high hedges. Public parks also have specific areas for those games not normally found in gardens, such as cricket, baseball, football and rugby.

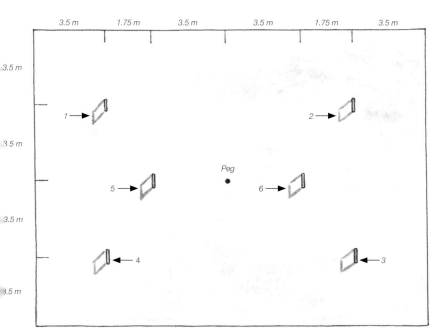

| 3.5 m | 1.75 m | 3.5 m | 3.5 m | 1.75 m | 3.5 m |

3.5 m

1 →

2 →

3.5 m

Peg

5 →

6 →

3.5 m

← 4

← 3

3.5 m

Croquet lawn

Although associated nostalgically in the popular imagination with endless Edwardian summer afternoons, croquet is still played in many countries, and nowhere more competitively than in the USA. Its forerunner, a game called crookey, arrived in England from Ireland in 1852 and quickly gained favour, spreading to many Commonwealth countries. It was one of the first outdoor sports in which women could compete with men on an equal footing, which may have accounted for its popularity at weekend country house parties.

Clip Art

Topiary is the art of clipping plants into ornamental shapes. It is an extreme example of the gardener's desire to 'reshape nature' as no tree or shrub grows into anything like the symmetrical forms found in topiary gardens. Dating back to Roman times or earlier, elaborate topiary was abundant in Pliny's garden at Tusci in the 2nd century AD and, to varying degrees, has never gone out of fashion since. When visiting gardens you will become familiar with common topiary designs such as cubes, balls, domes, pyramids, obelisks and bird and animal shapes.

Topiary poultry
As well as providing strong architectural form and structure to a garden, topiary can also amuse, delight or surprise the visitor.

Topiary shapes

The various geometric topiary shapes are often combined, for instance by cutting a dome on top of a cube or cylinder. As a topiary specimen becomes ever larger, the original shape is often distorted owing to the difficulty of clipping.

Spirals

One of the most complex shapes is the spiral, which truly challenges the skills of the topiary artist. The design involves winding string evenly around the tree to act as a cutting guide. The fine-leaved yew is a good subject for this method.

Tiers and lollipops

Small trees with single, straight trunks provide opportunities for complex tiered designs. 'Lollipop' shapes are also popular, involving a single, tall trunk with a clipped ball, box or heart cut into the canopy. Holly is often cut this way.

Animals

Fanciful topiary in the shape of animals has a long history and remains a favourite with topiary enthusiasts. Birds such as peacocks are a recurring theme and you will often see them sitting atop a yew hedge.

Versatile Hedges

On garden visits you will see many hedges of varying appearance that perform different functions. A tall hedge provides enclosure, shelter and protection, is much cheaper than building a wall and will last longer than a fence. They are as useful for edging a decorative parterre as for creating an impressive avenue. Evergreen hedges of yew, holly, box, laurel and privet are popular in formal gardens. Deciduous trees like hornbeam, beech and lime look good in country gardens, while flowering hedges such as rose, escallonia and hibiscus add great beauty to any garden.

Mien Ruys Garden, Dedemsvaart, the Netherlands
Here the innovative Dutch garden designer Mien Ruys (1904–99) has cleverly used a wall of miscanthus grass to echo the formal evergreen hedge behind.

French formality
Often a well-cut hedge imitates architecture very successfully. In grand French gardens they are shaped with such precision that they resemble walls, arches and niches far more than a row of trees. This yew hedge is shaped like a crenellated castle wall.

Dutch tradition
Throughout their history the Dutch have made much use of hedging as it thrives better than trees in the windswept Dutch landscape and its thin soils. At Het Loo a series of doorways and windows punctuate an avenue made entirely of hedging.

Japanese hedges

Camellia and holly are common hedging plants in Japan where you will see high hedges growing above walls or chunky bamboo fences. Similar tiered effects are achieved by creating a low hedge of one variety in front of a taller, contrasting one.

Country hedges

Rural gardens are often bounded by mixed hedges of native deciduous plants. In winter look for traditionally layered hedges where a stake cut from old wood is hammered into the ground and the rest of the hedge woven in, to create a thick barrier.

Garden Rooms

Sissinghurst Castle, Kent, England

Most gardens are only experienced on the ground level but, thanks to its viewing tower, the garden rooms at Sissinghurst can also be appreciated from on high.

Tall, dense hedging, commonly of yew or beech, is often used in gardens to create divisions and compartments you will often hear referred to as 'garden rooms'. These living walls give structure and form to a garden while the individual rooms afford the garden designer opportunities to experiment with different moods and themes. Look for rooms that contain a single group of specimens such as roses; ones organised by seasonal theme; those with restricted plantings of hot or cool colours; or that define areas of contrast such as lawns and ornamental beds.

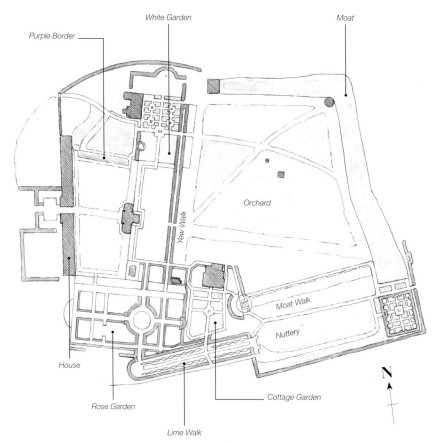

Purple Border

White Garden

Moat

Yew Walk

Orchard

Moat Walk

Nuttery

House

Rose Garden

Cottage Garden

Lime Walk

N

Plan of Sissinghurst

Vita Sackville-West's husband, Harold Nicolson (1886–1968), designed the layout of the gardens at Sissinghurst, beginning in the 1930s. The plan clearly shows how the liberal planting of hedges – hornbeam, boxwood and yew – cleverly augmented and extended the ruins of the original structure of brick walls. Note the dramatic vista created by tall, narrow hedges in the Yew Walk contrasting the adjacent open area of orchard. The intimate enclosures make the garden feel much larger than it is in reality.

Garden Puzzles

The origins of labyrinths and mazes (though not strictly correct, the terms are often used interchangeably) are lost in time. The earliest had mystical and symbolic significance and were simple flat shapes either cut into turf or outlined in brick or gravel. Some were even made of flowering plants like a simple parterre. The now familiar form of the hedge maze became popular in the 17th century; these are really a three-dimensional puzzle intended to thrill those who get lost within their confines. Large scale labyrinths or mazes were cut through woods.

Glendurgan Garden, Cornwall, England
Apart from the dubious delight and diversion of getting lost in a maze, if viewed from an elevated position they are also highly decorative.

Labyrinth
A true labyrinth is designed with a single path that is rational, if complicated, and leads to a single point. It is a symbolic representation of the religious ideal of the true path to purity that must be traversed through a sinful world.

Circular maze
Unlike the calm certainty of a true labyrinth, the inherent blind alleys of a maze offer the visitor frustration and exasperation! Since the Renaissance, mazes assumed a playful and decorative air, intended for diversion and entertainment.

Destination

At the centre of the maze (if the goal is reached) you often find a feature – perhaps a pavilion, fountain or tree. Some of the more elaborate have an elevated mound and a gazebo, or even a tower, for spying those still lost.

Plants

High, evergreen hedges provide walls that are impenetrable and are the best plants for obscuring all sense of location. However, some modern mazes are formed from much lighter materials such as bamboo or corn (hence the term 'maize maze').

The Invisible Boundary

The idea of a concealed barrier, separating the garden from bucolic nature beyond, is a concept derived from ancient Chinese gardening traditions. The ha-ha is a grassed ditch that creates the illusion of a rolling expanse of parkland by dispensing with all walls, hedges and fences. It was essential for creating the right prospect in 18th-century landscape parks. William Kent, Charles Bridgeman (1690–1738) and 'Capability' Brown all used the ha-ha in an attempt to reunite the garden with nature. Modern-day examples include the Washington Monument in the USA where the recently installed ha-ha keeps motor vehicles, rather than grazing sheep, at bay.

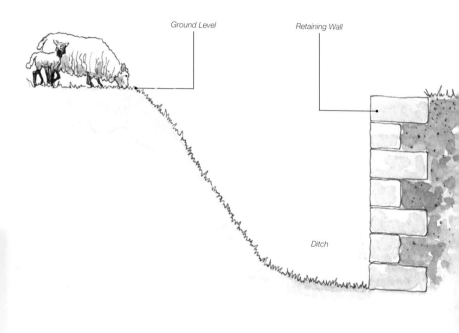

Ground Level

Retaining Wall

Ditch

The ha-ha

The ha-ha is a deeply sunk ditch or trench forming a barrier that is only visible at close quarters. Its construction has one elevation that gently slopes downwards (on the pasture side), while the other is a retaining wall of stone or brick (on the garden side). The aim is to keep grazing animals outside the park or garden without the need for fences, lending the scene a farm-like appearance. The term 'ha-ha' is thought to derive from the exclamations of surprise from unsuspecting strollers!

Prospects & Performances

Villa Rizzardi, Veneto, Italy
This green amphitheatre dates from the 18th century and forms part of a much larger garden designed by Luigi Trezza (1752–1823). Note the statues set within the hedge niches.

Reshaping a garden's terrain on any considerable scale requires space, finance and vision. An elevated prospect from which to view the garden and the world beyond is always much sought after. To this end you may discover the feature known as a bastion, an elevated walkway that ends in a vantage point. A different view is provided by a garden amphitheatre, an area devoted to outdoor performances. Based on designs for Classical amphitheatres, it consists of shallow stepped terraces, usually curved, cut into turf. Sometimes trees are planted as a backdrop.

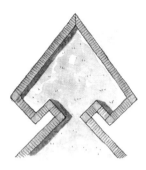

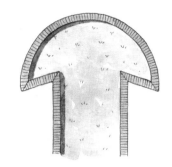

Arrowhead bastion

Traditionally bastions were built against, or at angles to, walls for fortification purposes. Their military associations made them a natural choice for inclusion in the gardens at the Duke of Marlborough's Blenheim Palace in Oxfordshire, England: it has eight.

Semi-circular bastion

Less thrusting than the previous arrowhead formation, the semi-circular bastion is more restful on the eye. Projecting out across the garden this bay affords the viewer the perfect place from which to appreciate the surrounding scene.

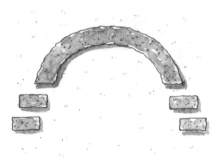

Amphitheatre

Open-air performances of plays and music sit well within the overall theatricality of a garden setting and are still popular. A new amphitheatre was created in the Englischer Garten in Munich, one of Europe's largest public parks, in 1985.

Outdoor theatres

Italian Renaissance villa gardens often had areas known as a *teatro di verdura*, or green theatre. Evergreen shrubs and trees were clipped to form backdrops and overlapping side wings, from which the players made their entrances and exits.

Mounds & Mounts

If you see an unnatural looking hill-like shape in a garden, chances are it will be a manmade mound or mount. These are intended to be climbed and will repay the effort with a wide, often panoramic, prospect across the garden below (especially knot designs and parterres) and the landscape beyond. Some are developed from the remains of old motte and bailey castles but many have been built from scratch. One of the most recent, and ambitious, is the viewing mount in Charles Jencks's Garden of Cosmic Speculation near Dumfries, Scotland.

West Wycombe Park, Bucks, England
The positioning of garden buildings on raised mounds enlarges the prospect for those within, and also enhances the significance of the building as a focal point in a garden.

Pyramid mound
The simplest mounds are small hills made of brick or stone, infilled with earth and turfed. Sometimes you will find them built in the shape of a pyramid. Medieval mounds acted as watchtowers in times of conflict and garden vantage points in peace.

Spiral mound
The spiral mound, also known as a snail mound, has a path cut into it that circumnavigates the hill, making the ascent (and descent) easier. Trees and shrubs may be planted on and around the mound and a summerhouse sited on top.

Stepped mound

Again for ease of ascent, steps are often set into the mound. These may be single steps set into the earth and staggered, or a more formal staircase. Look for doorways in the mound, which may conceal storage – even an icehouse.

Oriental mounds

Unlike the European model, which is intended to look artificial, Chinese and Japanese mounds mimic natural landscapes. Built of sandstone and concrete, and planted with trees and shrubs, they often feature grottoes and waterfalls.

Sunk Gardens

Packwood House, Warwickshire, England
The tiered effect of this sunken garden is exaggerated by the depression of the pool, the raised beds and the surrounding hedge.

The term 'sunk garden' applies to any garden that has been created in a depression. The change in level is usually quite shallow and not as obvious as the rising form of a mound. One of the best known is the Sunk Garden at Hampton Court, England, also referred to as the Pond or Dutch Garden (indicating that its sunken nature is not perhaps its most noticeable quality). Today many designers exploit subtle changes in levels to create special interest and contrast within a relatively small area.

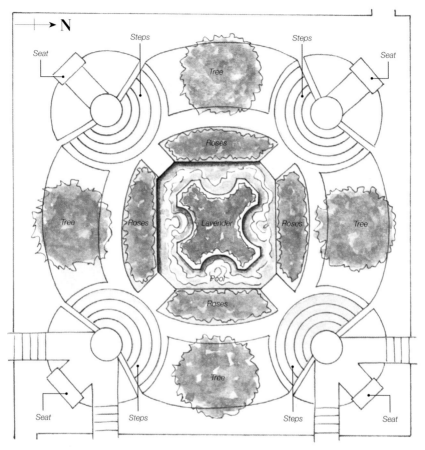

N

Seat · Steps · Steps · Seat
Tree
Roses
Roses · Lavender · Roses
Tree · Tree
Pool
Roses
Tree
Seat · Steps · Steps · Seat

Sunk garden, Folly Farm

Sunken garden rooms were a feature of many Arts and Crafts architects, among them Edwin Lutyens. Enclosed by yew hedges or walls the sunken garden was constructed using low terracing and often contained shallow ponds, rills or canals.

Lutyens created such a garden with a central pool at Folly Farm, Berkshire, England. At each of the four corners short flights of semi-circular steps rise to paved platforms containing seats. The restrained planting of roses and lavender is the work of Gertrude Jekyll.

Water, Water Everywhere

Water is a vital component of many gardens, irrespective of period or culture. A lake or large pond may have occurred naturally or be manmade. For clues to its origin, note the position and age of buildings, trees and other features in relation to it. Do they all appear as if conceived as a coherent composition, or do elements 'fit around' the water's edge? Can you detect the source (a spring, river or stream) or is the water a contained element? Is the overall shape regular (rectangular, round or oval) or irregular and more naturalistic? All may point to its origins.

Informal pool
A pool of water introduces new dimensions to a garden influencing the type of plants grown, while different species of wildlife may suddenly appear.

Moat

Originally moats were defensive barriers constructed around castles to keep out unwanted visitors. In later periods they became ornamental. You can still find them in many grand gardens where they lend an air of romance and historical association.

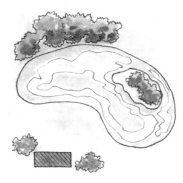

Position

Looking from the vantage point of the house, you often find lawns or formal gardens in the foreground, an expanse of water in the middle ground and woods or parkland beyond. This layout is typical of the landscape park.

Natural lake

This serpentine lake is fed by a stream so is likely to be natural, although some of its contours may have been reshaped. The damming and earth-moving required for making such 'improvements' on nature always denote great wealth.

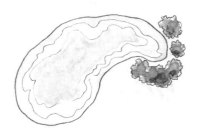

Artificial lake

A manmade lake always appears more convincing and natural if part of it is hidden from view. With this in mind, large clumps of trees or small woodlands are often strategically planted to shield the point at which the water ends.

Pools & Channels

Pools and ponds are far more modest than lakes, mostly manmade and often formal in shape. Small pools of water were vital ingredients in Roman gardens, as were the four converging channels in Islamic gardens in which water was regarded as the source of life. You will see many and varied types of ponds in gardens today, all displaying a wealth of historical and stylistic influences. Notice how a flat sheet of still water, of whatever size, provides a garden with a focal point and reflects the ever-changing movement of the sky above.

Garden in Greenwich, Connecticut, USA
Water holds the same fascination for contemporary designers as it did for their predecessors, as this garden by Oehme, van Sweden illustrates.

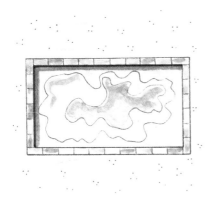

Canal
A canal is an artificial pool of flat, still water, usually rectangular, that varies greatly in size (the Grand Canal at Versailles is a mile long and unifies the entire garden). It may be functional (acting as a reservoir), purely decorative, or both.

Raised pond
Formal, symmetrical raised ponds have been popular since the Middle Ages and are still being made in modern gardens. Raising the pond proud of the ground brings the level of the water surface closer to the viewer's eye.

Japanese pond

In Japanese gardens ponds are constructed to resemble a particular type of landscape or scenery, such as an ocean, a marsh or river. The overall shape of the pond is partly obscured by rocks and planting; bridges and lanterns are common features.

Water parterre

In grand gardens you may find an elaborate water parterre. Very shallow pools of often florid and intricate designs are filled with coloured pebbles and then covered with water, creating a glistening version of the traditional parterre.

Aquatic Extravaganzas

Moving water brings a whole new dimension to the garden and nowhere is this better exploited than in the great Italian Renaissance gardens. The water gardens created around such grand houses as the Villas d'Este, Lante and Farnese are highly sophisticated feats of hydraulic engineering, as well as beautiful sculptural structures. See how water is used in an endlessly inventive array of cascades, fountains, pools, basins, troughs, jets and *giochi d'acqua*, or water jokes. These extravaganzas had a huge influence on later gardens, notably Louis XIV's Versailles.

Palace of Versailles, France
The mile-long Grand Canal terminates at the splendid Fountain of Apollo. While Apollo was god of the sun, Louis XIV was referred to as the sun king.

Basin fountain

The word fountain originates from *fons*, Latin for spring. The earliest were marble basins placed under natural springs to catch the water (later covered to prevent contamination). You will still see the simple basin shape, often mounted on a pedestal.

Pool fountain

The basin fountain has been elaborately developed over time. In a pool fountain, the water from the basin above overflows into a formal pool below, and is then pumped back up through the fountain by means of a circular pump.

Tiered fountain

By adding more than one basin, a tiered arrangement is achieved. Look for statuary and decorative stonework, resulting in a highly ornamental fountain. Mythical water nymphs, associated with natural springs, often adorn fountains.

Niche fountain

This is a variation on the tiered fountain, set within a niche or alcove. You will often see this in elaborate architectural schemes. One major advantage of this design is that all the hydraulics can be neatly hidden behind the façade of the niche.

Falling Water

Alnwick Garden, Northumberland, England
The Grand Cascade is one of the most ambitious water features recently created. During a 12-minute sequence 350 litres of water are ejected into the air every second!

Few garden water features are as impressive as a waterfall or a cascade. Both are about movement and sound but differ in construction. Most Japanese gardens contain at least one waterfall, its scale depending on the size of the garden, and it may be natural or manmade. They should always look natural. By contrast cascades are not intended to mimic nature, rather they aim to impress the viewer with their artifice and their sophisticated manipulation of such a natural element. Both denote status as they are expensive to install and maintain.

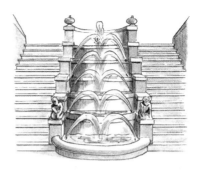

Cascade

You will find great formal cascades installed as part of grand, and costly, architectural schemes. Often sited on gently sloping ground, tiered steps further aid the rush of falling water. All pumping devices are hidden from view below ground.

Fountain cascade

Look for inventive variations in the design of cascades. Many widen towards the base while others are narrow and more steeply inclined, usually with steps either side. Extra interest and movement is sometimes added with multiple fountains.

Waterfall

There are many variations on the Japanese waterfall, and each has quite specific formations, the names of which describe how the water looks. In a front-falling waterfall the torrent falls evenly over rocks or a cliff edge in front of the viewer.

Stepped-falling waterfall

Another variation is the stepped-fall. When observing this type of waterfall note how the fall of the cascade is broken by protruding rocks, arranged like irregular steps. This formation creates extra drama as the water falls in unpredictable ways.

Water Jokes

In 16th-century Italy there was a fashion for water jokes and surprises, known as *giochi d'acqua*, and the craze spread to Russia, England and elsewhere in Europe. Water sources were concealed in statues, paths and other innocent-looking garden features that would suddenly emit fountains of water, drenching unsuspecting garden visitors (you have been warned!). A particularly elaborate example from the 17th century survives at the Hellbrunn Palace, Salzburg, Austria. Based on Greek mythology, the complex scheme includes water automata, grottoes and numerous fountains and water jets.

Hellbrunn Palace, Salzburg, Austria
With its 400-year-old trick fountains, Hellbrunn is still the best place to experience the thrill of fully functioning water jokes.

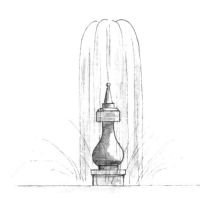

Surprise
Water jokes depend upon an element of surprise. Often they are hidden in a commonplace item such as a sundial. When the unsuspecting visitor pauses to check the position of the sun, a sprinkling of water shoots from a central spout.

Taste
In the 16th century it would not be considered crude or distasteful for a garden visitor to encounter a statue of a sweet chubby *putto* whose penis suddenly lifts and spouts water in their face; rather this would be thought a huge joke!

Engineering

As with elaborate fountains and cascades, water jokes require high levels of engineering and continual maintenance (hence few survive). Some were operated by manual switches but could also be triggered by the footfall of the casual passer-by.

Artifice

At Chatsworth, Derbyshire, England, the 1826 replica of a copper willow tree can still be seen (the original dated from 1693). From the branches of this beautifully crafted tree water rains down on visitors, evoking surprise and delight.

Wellheads

The well was commonly the central feature of Roman courtyards and appears in numerous woodcuts of medieval cloister gardens. Italian Renaissance wellheads in marble or carved stone are especially beautiful. Over the centuries many have been exported so you are likely to see them in several countries, used as impressive focal points in formal gardens. Spanish versions were usually constructed of brick or stone and faced with decorative tiles. Occasionally you may come across a wellhouse, which is a small building built over the wellhead, but these are unusual.

Wellhead

Wellheads may be simple or ornate in design. Many of the more elaborate are based on the form of capitals, or incorporate frieze-like figures and animals. Imported wellheads are often positioned for effect rather than function, with no well beneath.

Overthrow

An overthrow is a device for supporting the pulley rope or chain and bucket over an open wellhead. Overthrows can be made of wrought iron or stone and are usually quite ornate.

American wellheads

Colonial American wellheads have integral roofs incorporated into their structure but remain open at the sides. The top of the well has a wooden cover. These structures are attractive as well as functional and are often found close to the house.

Dipping well

A dipping well is a small circular pool with a semi-circular dome above. A wall-mounted fountain feeds the pool. You will see these on the terraces of several Arts and Crafts gardens. Originally watering cans were dipped in for filling.

Rills

A rill is a small stream or brook that has been channelled through a garden. Most commonly they are straight but you may occasionally see one that gently meanders for a more informal effect. They derive from the four 'river' channels – the *charbagh* – of Islamic gardens, then later formed part of the elaborate water schemes in Italian and French gardens. In Spanish and Dutch gardens they are referred to as canals. A recurring motif in Arts and Crafts gardens, rills are currently enjoying something of a revival among contemporary designers.

Hackel Garden, Lucerne, Switzerland
Commonly rills are found set into an expanse of flat lawn. Here the rill is bordered by a dense planting of moisture-loving plants.

Plan of East Rill, Hestercombe Gardens, Taunton, England
One of the most celebrated rills is that designed in 1904–6 by Edwin Lutyens at Hestercombe Gardens, Somerset, England. They are in fact a pair of rills, positioned to the east and west of the area known as the Great Plat. Each is generously edged with Ham Hill stone. The planting scheme was by Gertrude Jekyll and the whole garden now represents one of the best restored examples of her work.

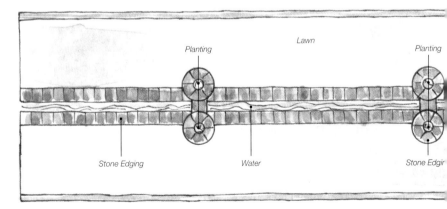

Planting   Lawn   Planting

Stone Edging   Water   Stone Edgir

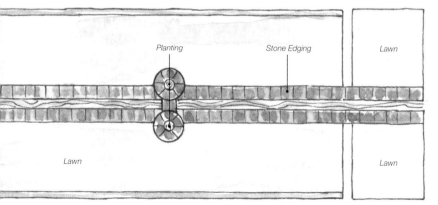

Planting

Stone Edging

Lawn

Lawn

Lawn

Lawn

Functional & Fanciful

Introduction

Manoir d'Eyrignac, Dordogne, France
This handsome 18th-century pavilion not only provides an architecturally sympathetic poolside changing area but, more importantly, acts as a focal point for the garden's layout.

Buildings are very important features of many gardens. Identifying the type of structure, its style and quality of construction, will help you to access the status, wealth and aspirations of the garden's owner, as well as provide some valuable historical context. The appeal of built covered structures seems universal, as they appear in gardens all over the world and from all periods. You will find they vary widely, from the grand to the humble, and from the purely decorative to the seriously functional, but all are of interest to the garden visitor.

Function

Consider whether the building before you has a function. It may give shelter (to people or plants), divert the eye, express wealth, or simply offer the best possible prospect from which to enjoy a view.

Identification

The question 'What is this?' is not always easy to answer. Is it a gazebo, a pavilion, a summerhouse, or a poolhouse? Indeed, it may be all these things and confusingly the terms often seem interchangeable.

Style

Garden buildings can be quite eccentric. Their treatment is often less serious than that lavished on the main building; they are not always architecturally correct, and they do not necessarily relate to local cultural traditions or materials.

Purpose

The original purpose of a building may well have changed over time. In a garden open to the public an orangery may now be a café, while elsewhere what was a shepherd's hut is now a summerhouse and an old lavatory a tool store.

Temples of Delight

Temples are among the grandest buildings you will find in a garden. Although closely associated with the English landscape park, you will also see them in many other situations. They are always roofed but the sides may be enclosed or open and are large enough to house several visitors comfortably. Many have a colonnade surmounted by a pediment. You will find variations on this model, such as the Temple of British Worthies at Stowe, Buckinghamshire, England, which is actually a series of connected temples, each containing a niche for the display of portrait busts.

Stourhead, Wiltshire, England
The Pantheon is the grandest of several temples positioned around the landscape at Stourhead. Others here are dedicated to the gods Apollo and Flora.

Position
Temples are expensive buildings to install. Take note of their position as they will always have been placed within a garden for maximum effect, perhaps framed by specimen trees or reflected in a lake.

Orders
Many temples are faithful copies of Classical originals, though you will also find ones that are inventive conflations of structural and decorative elements. This temple pairs Ionic columns with a segmental pediment.

Style

Hybrid styles are sometimes applied to temple structures. Gothic interpretations are far more decorative than their Classical counterparts, with heavy ornamentation. The architectural style of a temple will not necessarily reflect that of the main building.

Construction

The highest quality temples are made from marble or cut stone; others are rendered, built in brick or sometimes a mixed palette of materials may be used. The roof can be tiled or, especially if it is domed, may be formed from lead.

Other Eye-catching Edifices

Chastleton Glebe, Oxfordshire, England
This delicate pagoda strikes an oriental note in this English garden. The eastern effect is further enhanced by the Japanese-style bridge.

The types of building referred to as a rotunda or a pagoda strike a more playful note in the garden than the more austere Classical temple. A rotunda – basically a circular ring of columns crowned with a domed roof – is smaller than a temple and open at the sides. If you see a closed rotunda, it is likely to be based on the Temple of Vesta at Tivoli, Italy, or Bramante's famous Tempietto at Rome. Chinese-inspired pagodas were very popular in 18th-century gardens, just as oriental motifs were fashionable for interior decoration.

Design

Look for variations in design, such as arches surmounted on square columns, rusticated stonework and ornate pinnacles added to the domed roof. Occasionally the openings are glazed, making the structure weatherproof and therefore more functional.

Rotunda

Although a rotunda may be useful if a visitor is caught in an unexpected shower, the classic form of this building has little functional use. Rather they act as a focal point, or eye-catcher, in a landscape, and are best viewed from afar.

Pagoda

The pagoda at Kew Gardens, London, is an authentic copy of a Chinese original. Set within gardens such tall, tiered, octagonal buildings were an arresting sight. The number of storeys may differ – Kew's has ten – but all afford far-reaching views.

Style

Following the construction of the pagoda at Kew (1761) oriental-style buildings began to appear in many gardens throughout Europe. Their scale and the faithfulness of architectural detail vary considerably, but all add an air of playfulness, frivolity and decorative charm.

Gloomy Grottoes

The concept of the grotto dates back to the nymphaeum of Greek and Roman times, a damp and shady place where offerings were made to nymphs. The idea enjoyed a revival in Renaissance Italy and they were common in grand gardens across Europe by the mid-16th century. While the interior is cave-like and mysterious, the outer façade is usually architecturally formal. By contrast British grottoes are often naturalistic inside and out. A grotto may be natural or completely artificial (or a combination) and, although cool and shady in the heat of summer, their prime purpose is symbolic.

Arboretum Trsteno, near Dubrovnik, Croatia
With Neptune centre stage, flanked by two water nymphs, this grotto is a baroque-style reconstruction dating from 1736. An earlier version was damaged in an earthquake.

Chinese grotto
Chinese grottoes are far less elaborate than European versions. Oddly shaped rocks are assembled into artificial arrangements that symbolise sacred mountains. Imbued with Taoist and magical meanings, they become places of reflection and retreat.

Gothic grotto
Although the exterior of some grottoes appears as little more than a craggy entrance to a cave, many present a more formal face to the world. This gothic-style grotto has windows as well as a doorway and is patterned with stone- and shellwork.

Niche grotto

Note the scale; some grottoes are large cavern-like networks of passages, while others are little more than a niche set in a wall or among shrubs. Water is a vital element here, and may be provided by a natural spring or pumped from a pool.

Construction

Look closely to see if a grotto is natural, manmade or a combination. Natural materials include flints, fossils and tufa (a compressed volcanic ash). These will be embellished with shells, inset with mirrors and augmented with fake stalactites.

Elevated Viewing

Originally a gazebo was an elevated small structure that overlooked a garden. It might be open-sided or enclosed, square, octagonal or shaped to fit in a corner. They were also positioned on a mound at the centre of a maze, and the term still refers to a building in which to sit and enjoy a view from a high position. The word gazebo may be a conflation of the Latin *'ebo'* and *'gaze'*, resulting in 'I shall gaze'. Confusingly it is now freely applied to any garden structure intended for sitting in.

T'ing

The Chinese version of the gazebo is known as a t'ing. Usually open-sided it sits on three steps and is positioned on higher ground, on a bridge or by the side of a pond, wherever a view can be best enjoyed.

Kiosk

A kiosk is a, usually smaller, variant of the gazebo. Its design adheres to no particular style; indeed you can find a mix of Moorish, Arabic and oriental influences applied with little or no rigour or consistency!

Rusticity

Gazebos constructed from rustic timber, often thatched or with shingle roof tiles, were very popular in 19th-century public parks and domestic gardens, especially in Britain. Attractive Swiss and German chalet-style structures were also favoured.

Trelliswork

Open trellis continues to be used for creating light and airy 'walls' around gazebos. It provides shade and a level of privacy without obscuring the view. Suitable alternative materials are wooden fretwork and ornate wrought iron.

Flights of Fancy

Unlike most garden buildings, a folly has no practical use whatsoever. It is part of that strong tradition of theatricality and fantasy that belongs to much garden making. In the 18th century, the height of the fashion for follies, numerous fake structures built to resemble castles, towers, hermitages or fragmentary ruins were hastily constructed in fashionable gardens all over Europe. These constructions were intended to evoke surprise, delight or simple puzzlement in the unsuspecting garden visitor, especially if they caught a fleeting glimpse of a hirsute hermit!

Folly, near Ardcath, County Meath, Ireland
Although providing an elevated viewing point, and acting as an eye-catcher, this building is as functionless – if attractive – as most follies.

Folly

The ultimate functionless garden building is a completely new structure built to resemble a tumbledown ruin. (In the 18th century the irony is unlikely to have been lost on the labourers whose own dwellings were often inadequate.) Folly indeed!

Ruin

Note a ruin's architectural style as this may express particular ideals associated with patriotism or aesthetics. Archaeological fragments, ruined castles, sham cloisters convey a different set of associations: romantic, chivalrous or perhaps penitent.

Hermitage

This building is intended to resemble a hermit's cell. It is a primitive hut with an earth floor (more macabre versions are paved with the bones of sheep and cows), partly obscured by trees so the visitor is surprised by the unexpected encounter.

Root house

One of the more extreme variations on the hermitage is the root house, a grotesque hut constructed from giant twisted roots, hardly fit for habitation. The English aristocracy and gentry were especially fond of such whimsical structures.

Far Pavilions

Yet another group of garden buildings is encompassed by the term summerhouse or, sometimes, garden pavilion. The summerhouse is more functional than a temple or gazebo and comes in many guises, including fishing huts (by lakes), sports pavilions (alongside bowling greens, tennis courts, etc) and poolhouses (close to swimming pools with facilities for changing). The summerhouse can also be a place of work, and many writers have retreated to garden rooms to think and create, among them George Bernard Shaw and Virginia Woolf.

Formal summerhouse
Summerhouses may be positioned for privacy and retreat. Although rather grand for its purpose, this poolside garden pavilion promises peace and solitude.

Summerhouse
A summerhouse may be partly open or completely enclosed. The former design provides shade in summer (sometimes called a shadow house), while the latter is more functional in cooler climates. As with garden temples, it may differ in style to the main house.

Pavilion
Pavilions and summerhouses have traditionally been associated with retreat and recreation. In the great gardens of 17th-century France they represented an escape from the formality of court life (although by any standards these buildings were still highly elaborate).

Teahouse

Teahouses feature in many Japanese gardens, some of which date back to the 16th century. These buildings consist of an open waiting room and an enclosed teahouse where visitors gather to partake of the formal tea-drinking ceremony, which is considered an aesthetic experience.

Tent

The fashion for garden tents came to Europe in the Middle Ages when the returning Crusaders introduced oriental-style temporary pole and cloth structures to the garden to provide shade. Eighteenth-century versions were sometimes made of tin, formed and painted to resemble canvas.

Other Garden Houses

The garden visitor encounters a considerable array of buildings whose purpose is not always immediately apparent. However, a great number of these do fulfil a proper function, or certainly did in the past. Whether they be gate, banqueting, boat, ice, smoke or bathhouses, architects have often viewed the construction of such places as an opportunity for playful disguise. Those buildings located closest to the house will have greatest domestic use (hence the need for disguise) while those found further away are less likely to be required daily.

The Swiss Garden, Bedfordshire, England
This charming little Swiss cottage (complete with chimney) provides the focal point for the garden designed by Lord Ongley in the 1820s for his Swiss mistress.

Gatehouse
Gatehouses always denote wealth and status. Commonly found at the entrance to the park or estate of a grand house, they enabled the gatekeeper to monitor all incomers. You will also find a gatehouse closer to smaller country houses, usually at the entrance to a courtyard.

Banqueting house
Many of the grand houses of Europe that date from the Renaissance period had separate banqueting houses located within their gardens. The hosts and guests would retire here to enjoy after-dinner wine and sweet things while admiring the grounds from elevated rooms.

Boathouse

Situated alongside a lake or river, in large and grand gardens you will often see very impressive buildings to house rowing boats, punts or canoes. These lovely examples of architectural fancies appear in a wide variety of styles and may incorporate a summerhouse above the moorings.

Icehouse

Icehouses, made of brick or stone then packed with ice, were often set below ground to increase the insulation. These garden larders were for storing perishables before the era of refrigeration, but their function did not prevent them from becoming another vehicle for architectural excess.

The View on High

Sissinghurst Castle, Kent, England
Imposing and substantial structures, like towers, often pre-date their surrounding garden, such as the one at Sissinghurst, which is Elizabethan.

Belvederes and towers are among the most conspicuous buildings found in gardens. The word belvedere is Italian for 'beautiful to see' and refers to a high structure, often a tower, affording spectacular views. Known as watch towers or prospect towers, many originally served a defensive function and were later commandeered for pleasurable purposes. However, others have been built just to impress, and dominate a landscape visually for great distances. The intention is that such buildings should be looked at, as well as looked from, serving as eye-catchers or focal points.

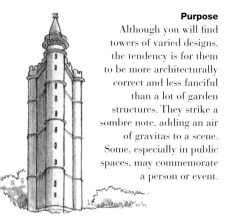

Purpose

Although you will find towers of varied designs, the tendency is for them to be more architecturally correct and less fanciful than a lot of garden structures. They strike a sombre note, adding an air of gravitas to a scene. Some, especially in public spaces, may commemorate a person or event.

Style

Towers may be Classical, gothic, round, square, pointed or castellated in design. They vary in height considerably and are often positioned on high ground, further accentuating their importance. The higher the tower, the more affluent its owner.

Clock tower

As its name suggests, a clock tower is a tower with at least one clock face set within its structure. Many have four, one on each façade, thus enabling the time to be seen at a distance from multiple viewpoints.

Location

Clock towers are more common in public parks than private gardens, although small clock towers can be incorporated into other functional garden buildings such as gatehouses or stable blocks.

Gardens in Glass

A glass- or greenhouse is a utilitarian building, most often found within, or close to, working areas such as the kitchen garden. They protect tender plants from cold and damp conditions while their glass roofs allow maximum light. Although the idea dates back to Roman times, in Europe glasshouses became common in large gardens in the 17th century, some of grand scale and design. By the 1800s small greenhouses were available to domestic and amateur gardeners in all regions where the weather presented a threat. They are vital tools in the gardener's campaign to extend which plants can be grown, when and where.

Greenhouse interior
Think of the greenhouse as the engine room at the heart of a garden, its purpose to raise tender plants and protect them from the elements, thereby extending the growing season.

Lean-to greenhouse
In large domestic gardens you are more likely to see one or two lean-to greenhouses, built against a high garden wall. These are often very attractive buildings so may be positioned in more visible areas than large estate glasshouses.

Glasshouses
A range of extensive glasshouses is essential for propagating a sufficiently large stock of plants to furnish an impressive garden throughout the seasons, with each house providing a particular combination of heat, light, ventilation and humidity to suit certain plant types.

Lean-to cold frame

Glass- and greenhouses may be heated or not but cold frames, as their name suggests, never are. Tender potted plants are placed in the frames to acclimatise to outdoor conditions before being planted. This is known as 'hardening off'.

Free-standing cold frame

Whether built against a wall (often of a greenhouse) or free-standing, essentially a cold frame is a brick or wooden box with removable glazed panels. The panels are partially or wholly removed by day then replaced at night as temperatures fall.

Specialist Houses

Purpose-built peachhouse
In this perfectly restored and maintained peachhouse nectarines blossom and flourish in ideal environmental conditions: the correct temperature, humidity and light are essential.

Among those buildings collectively known as glass- or greenhouses you will find those devoted to the cultivation of a particular type of flower or fruit. These include vineries (grapes), pineries (pineapples), orangeries (citrus fruit), palmhouses, peachhouses, cherryhouses and fighouses, each designed to provide the best possible conditions to promote (or force) the most prolific flowering or ripening of fruit. Note how light, temperature, ventilation and the area available for root expansion all vary, according to the crop grown. By contrast a mushroomhouse (or shed) is a dark affair, with all light excluded.

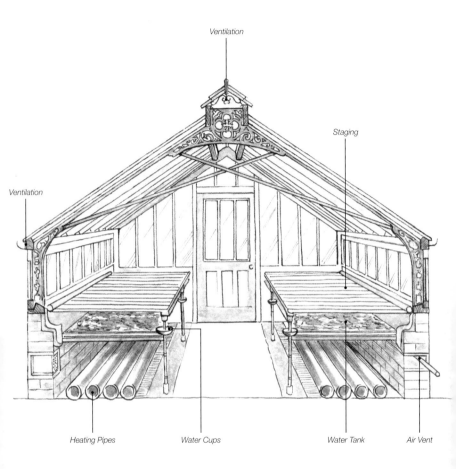

Ventilation

Ventilation

Staging

Heating Pipes _Water Cups_

Water Tank _Air Vent_

Orchidhouse

The complexity shown in this cross-section of an orchidhouse, dating from around 1900, illustrates the care taken in the design and construction of a building solely intended for the raising of one type of tender flower. Notice how air enters from side vents and is then warmed as it circulates over the hot pipes at ground level. Water cups near the top of the iron upright rails prevent ravaging pests such as slugs from reaching the plants, while the shallow water tanks under the wooden staging raise levels of humidity.

Glass Palaces

Glass- and greenhouses are for plants, whereas conservatories, although filled with plants, are primarily intended for people. You see them in private and public gardens, of varying sizes and designs, ranging from free-standing large botanical showcases to intimate domestic glazed rooms attached to a house. Many have deep beds for growing large specimens. A Winter Garden is a large glasshouse (sometimes with a solid rather than a glazed roof) that was devised during the 19th century, often as part of the schemes for public parks and leisure resorts. People were encouraged to stroll here in inclement weather to admire the attractive displays of plants.

The Royal Botanic Garden, Edinburgh, Scotland
When building was complete in 1858 Edinburgh's Temperate Palm House had cost £6,000 (which is equivalent today to over a quarter of a million pounds).

Materials

Technical developments in cast and wrought iron and the invention of plate glass in the 19th century enabled the construction of elaborate and affordable conservatories (also helped, in Britain, by the abolition of the glass tax in 1845.)

Condition

Note the age and condition of a botanical conservatory. Is it original, heavily restored or a replica of an earlier example? Given their purpose, all conservatories are especially vulnerable to decay as well as being expensive to maintain and to heat.

Position

Smaller conservatories constructed against a dwelling often fare better in terms of condition, as they are maintained along with the house. They are mostly sited on the south and southeast of a building to take full advantage of the sun's heat and light.

Design

A free-standing conservatory carries less architectural 'responsibility' but, to ensure aesthetic harmony, one that is attached to the house should echo its building style. The decorative design of this gothic structure is a clue to its non-functionality.

Opulent Orangeries

Karlsaue, Kassel, Germany
The Landgrave Karl had this ornate orangery built in 1710 as the centrepiece to his new baroque gardens. In addition to housing citrus trees, in 1747 it was briefly home to a rhinoceros named Clara!

An orangery is a high-status building only found in gardens of wealth and position. Prior to the air freighting of foods from around the world, oranges and other citrus fruits were great delicacies in cooler climates. Their cultivation demanded expertise and the provision of suitable growing conditions, achieved by housing the trees indoors in heated orangeries over the winter, then placing them outdoors in huge pots during summer. Although designs vary, the orangery is a coherent and easily recognisable type of building, characterised by large airy rooms and high windows to let in light.

Function

Such is the elegance of the orangery that during summer months, when empty of citrus, they have traditionally been used for entertaining. As the fashion (and necessity) for citrus cultivation has waned, many have been turned into sculpture courts or exhibition spaces.

Construction

Orangeries are far more imposing than glasshouses or conservatories and their construction is always more substantial. They are roofed and usually designed to reflect the architectural style of the main building. Mostly they are set within formal gardens, often amid pools, lawns and topiary.

Cultivation

The most elaborate citrus containers featured collapsible sides. A hinged construction enabled the gardener to root-prune the tree without needing to remove it from its pot. Skill and attention were required to keep a citrus tree healthy and fruiting.

Containers

For ease of transfer, citrus trees were grown in large wooden or ceramic containers. These were often of very beautiful design as they formed part of the garden's display in the summer months. Many incorporated loops for attaching carrying rods.

Bothy Boys

Tucked into an unpromising corner or tacked onto the side of a kitchen garden wall, you occasionally come across a small and simple building that does not seem to conform to other types of garden building. In former times this is likely to have provided accommodation for an under-gardener. This humble dwelling, known as the 'bothy', was commonly located at the functional heart of the garden. While plants basked in the warmth and light of the south-facing glasshouse, the young, unmarried male gardener shivered in his hut on the north side of the same wall!

Garden hut
Today many of the structures that once provided hovel-like accommodation for lowly gardeners have been converted into bijou garden huts, complete with decorative trim and climbing flowers.

Accommodation
Gardeners' accommodation varied widely. In the better establishments the head gardener dwelt in a house, an under-gardener in a worker's cottage (often near or above stable blocks) and an 'improver' (young apprentice) in the bothy.

Position
In gardens with heated glasshouses the bothy would be close to the boilerhouse. On cold winter nights the boiler fires required regular stoking (by the garden boy) to ensure that the hothouses were kept at a constant temperature.

Condition

Many bothies have now fallen into a ruinous state, or have been converted to become tool or potting sheds. Note the contrast of conditions on either side of this garden wall; one displays an elegant urn, the other a primitive hut!

Propriety

As women began to enter the horticultural profession in the early 20th century, employers had to upgrade the provided accommodation. Young educated women were less willing either to live in the traditional bothy, or share with the boys.

Architectural Detail

Introduction

Architectural garden features are among the many things you encounter in a garden that are not plants, landscape features or garden buildings. They may vary in scale from a bridge across a lake to a flower-filled urn; they may be functional, such as a wall, or purely decorative, like a statue. Such features contribute to the texture and atmosphere of a garden. The level and quality of detail applied to them tells you much about the care, attention and cost lavished on the project by the original garden maker and their condition demonstrates how subsequent custodians have maintained them.

Urn and colonnade
A well-chosen feature, such as this elegant urn, can be used to great effect to set the tone and mood of a garden.

Style
A great variety of different styles are applied to a host of architectural features, such as columns. Some perform a function, for instance as support for a pergola, while others are decorative only. Ask yourself why this particular style was chosen.

Purpose
Even the most seemingly innocuous item can express meaning. A garden gate, for instance, conveys a quite different message if it is open or ajar than if it is closed and bolted. Gates can welcome you into the space beyond, or bar your entrance.

Intention

The style and content of a feature such as a piece of sculpture may impart gravitas or humour. Note also whether a feature is appropriate to its setting, or whether its presence is jarring.

Permanence

Note where and how evolving changes in fashion have been incorporated into a garden. It is far easier (and cheaper) to change an item like a seat or a plant container than to alter the layout of a garden or the style of a summerhouse.

Ornament & Decoration

Historically, certain decorative styles have tended to be dominant in the garden, just as in architecture. You will frequently see these applied as surface pattern on all kinds of items. Consider the following: is the choice of design appropriate? Is it consistent with the surrounding buildings? Does it relate to the locality or show foreign influence? Also, note whether it is consistent with the age of the garden or is an anachronism. The use of pattern offers the garden maker another opportunity to introduce playfulness and theatricality into a scene.

The oriental touch
A recurring characteristic of Chinese and Japanese ornament is its great delicacy, as evident in this delightful bridge.

Persian
It is hard to overemphasise the influence of early Islamic gardens on subsequent designers. However, outside those countries with Moorish connections, it is the form of the garden, rather than its ornamentation, that most persists.

Oriental
Well beyond the gardens of China and Japan, you will encounter many and varied applications of oriental-style pattern and decoration. These range from large structures such as a moon gate or bridge to smaller features like furniture.

Classical

Greek and Roman designs, and their later reinterpretations, have provided the main palette for numerous garden makers in many countries. The patterns are elaborate and complex, often interwoven with mythical beasts and cherubic figures.

Gothic

On your travels you will see ornate gothic designs applied to everything from window frames to plant pots. Traditionally very popular in British gardens and based on natural plant forms, the style has a close affinity with rustic garden features.

Columns

A column is a tall, often circular, pillar, usually of stone though some are carved from wood. Those of a simpler design may be rectangular or square in plan and made from brick. You will find columns in gardens from many cultures. They are used structurally and decoratively as part of all kinds of garden buildings, for instance temples or around the cloisters in courtyard gardens. You frequently see them deployed supporting crossbeams for pergolas and loggias. Occasionally they perform no function other than as an ornament in a setting.

Courtyard garden, Campeche, Mexico
Columns are an important architectural feature of the cloister around this contained courtyard garden, providing shade and privacy.

The Orders

The European Classical language of architecture is based on the ancient Greek and Roman model. Essential to this are what are known as the Orders. These are columns with a base (most often), shaft, capital and entablature (the cornice, frieze and architrave). Each element is decorated and precisely proportioned to set rules. You will see columns that conform to these designs in gardens all over the world – although their use does not always adhere strictly to the Classical rules of architecture and can be subverted for effect (or they may simply be used incorrectly).

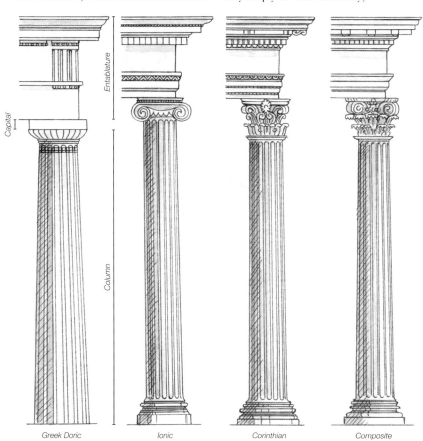

Greek Doric   *Ionic*   *Corinthian*   *Composite*

Green Arcades

Many gardens contain one or more examples of the group of architectural features known variously as loggias, pergolas, arbours, bowers and galleries. Although the name and design may differ, all provide shade, a degree of privacy and are usually situated to take full advantage of a view or vista. They are also attractive supports for climbing plants. The most impressive of the group is the pergola, a Renaissance revival of a Classical model. This became a staple feature of Arts and Crafts gardens and is still popular today.

Timberframe pergola
In summer a pergola is fragrant and lush with climbing plants, while in winter its frame presents a much starker architectural presence.

Loggia
A loggia is a row of columns forming a cloister or arcade. Open on one side, it is usually attached to a building, although in gardens you may sometimes find a loggia constructed along the length of a garden wall.

Pergola
'Pergola', from the Latin *pergula*, a projection, is a double row of substantial upright columns or posts supporting a network of crossbeams. It is open to the sky with a square, arched or ogee-shaped (a shallow reverse curve) profile.

Arbour

Rather confusingly the terms arbour and bower seem interchangeable. Smaller than a loggia or pergola, these shelters are open at the top and sides, provide support for climbing plants and usually house a seat. Their design varies according to situation.

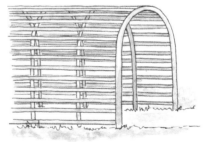

Gallery

The gallery is another variation on this group of structures. Think of a gallery as an arched green tunnel of climbing plants, supported on a light framework that is usually made of iron or wood, sometimes in the form of trelliswork.

Obelisks & Uprights

Obelisks, colonnades and eye-catchers impart height and formality to a scene. Whether used singly or arranged in a rhythmic sequence, their effectiveness relies on tall, slim shapes so it is natural that they are often variations on the Classical column form. For maximum impact they must be set within plenty of space and where their effect can be appreciated from afar. Great care will have been taken in positioning these features so note if they terminate a vista for instance, or draw the eye away from a less engaging view. A particularly large eye-catcher may be adapted for reasons of status or power from what was previously a defensive structure, such as a lookout tower.

Isola Bella, Lake Maggiore, Italy
The extreme elevated positions of this finial-topped obelisk and the neighbouring sculptural figure ensures maximum visibility from near and from afar.

Colonnade

A colonnade is a regularly spaced single row of columns. In gardens these are most usually freestanding, unconnected by any entablature (unlike those integral to a building). Columnar-shaped trees, such as cypress and Irish yews, are sometimes planted in colonnades and may be clipped or simply rely on their upright form.

Obelisk

An obelisk is a tapering pillar, usually of stone, set on a four-sided, triangular, circular or octagonal base. Popular in ancient Rome, the obelisk enjoyed a revival as an architectural feature in Italian and French formal gardens. Look out for a commemorative inscription.

Exedra

Particularly popular in 18th-century landscape gardens, the exedra is a semi-circular backdrop arranged rather like an apse in a church. These are formed from rows of columns, arches or a series of connected niches, or occasionally a combination of architecture and hedging.

Eye-catcher

As the name suggests, an eye-catcher is any very noticeable feature that catches and focuses the viewer's attention. Whether a tower, column or sculpture, it is position that is paramount. To achieve sufficient distance from the observer they may be placed outside the garden's boundary.

Boundary Markers

Every garden you visit has its parameters, whether apparent or not. Each is contained – by walls, fences, ditches, moats, hedges, woodlands or other structures. The garden boundary is directly connected to many of the recurring themes in this book – such as ownership, privacy, enclosure, display – all these ideas are expressed within or by physical perimeters. Consider whether a boundary is closed (such as an impenetrable high wall, fence or hedge) or open (edged only by a ha-ha, or an open-work fence), as this tells you much about the owner's attitudes towards the world outside.

Walled gardens
Although often obscured in part by plants, a boundary such as this wall demarcates the important transition point between the garden within and the world beyond.

Solid wall

Solid walls are constructed of many types of materials, most commonly brick and stone. They vary in height but a substantial wall around a garden always denotes wealth and imparts a sense of permanence, offering privacy and exclusion.

Crinkle-crankle wall

Walls provide excellent protection and support for many plants. Look out for undulating crinkle-crankle walls, also known as serpentine walls. Each bay creates a mini microclimate offering extra protection for tender plants.

Coping

A wall of quality will often be capped at the top, known as coping. Numerous designs for coping may be incorporated into garden walls, some often quite elaborate, such as the complex castellation here. Such non-standard construction is costly.

Chinese coping

Oriental gardens have wide and solid walls with very distinctive coping. Typically these are formed from little peaked roofs with wide overhanging curved eaves. Note the frequent use of coloured glazed tiles, which may also be inset into the wall.

Open Edging

An open boundary, one that you can literally see through or over, presents an altogether more inviting face to the visitor than a high solid wall. Variations in construction and design are numerous, although more substantial materials such as strong timber, iron or open brickwork are usually used for perimeter boundaries. Lighter weight, open-work fencing – latticework, trelliswork and ornamental wrought iron – is often found within the garden, which can be successfully used to create divisions or screen unwanted views. Wooden fencing is the least expensive but also shorter lived than the alternatives.

Cottage-style fencing
Although of simple construction, this wooden fence enhances this garden scene, providing an element of structure amid a jungle of flowering plants.

Picket fence
The neat wooden picket fence frames many a garden but is especially associated with North American plots. Painted white, you will see endless design variations for the pickets (uprights), rails (horizontals) and finials (ornamental tops).

Iron fencing
Iron fencing (also known as railing) became popular in the 19th century. Elaborate designs may incorporate bespoke detail such as a coat of arms or entwined initials. More often associated with town and city gardens, they usually enclose formal areas.

Trelliswork

Developed from simple latticework fencing trelliswork (*treillage* in French) is open wooden fencing, often of a highly complex design. As well as fencing or screening an area, it is used in decorative architectural structures and also to support plants.

Clairvoyee

The device known as a *clairvoyee* is a perfect example of an open boundary used within a garden. It is an ornate ironwork panel, set within a wall or hedge, which allows the viewer to look beyond but not to pass through it.

Making an Entrance

Biscainhos Palace Garden, Braga, Portugal

A finely constructed and highly ornamental gate pier that certainly conforms to Jekyll's maxim: one yearns to know what marvels await the visitor within.

Gertrude Jekyll wrote. 'A good gateway should put the stranger into the state of mind in which he will see what he approaches to the best advantage: it should excite him and prepare him like the overture of an opera.' You will encounter all types of garden gates, from the grandest with its gate house to the humblest with its broken latch. However, do be aware that, due to the necessity of managing visitor traffic, many gardens no longer use their original entrance. Sadly, all too often you enter by the back gate, rather than the front!

Classical gateway

The original purpose of a gateway was enclosure as well as fortification from the outside world and these ideas continued to be expressed visually if not physically in garden designs. This gateway conveys strength and power, although the actual gate is merely ornamental.

Piers

Gate piers have provided architects with numerous opportunities for creating elaborate theatrical entrances to gardens and estates. Note how they are often topped with fancy finials, sculpted heraldic beasts like griffins or, as here, oversized ornamental urns.

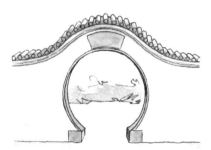

Moon gate

A moon gate (also known as a moon door) is a circular aperture set within a wall in traditional Chinese gardens. The best examples are topped with ceramic tiles that end in designs of talismans, each with its own symbolic meaning.

Lych gate

A lych gate is a gateway with a substantial roof, often incorporating simple seating into its design. Originally found only at the entrance to churchyards, they became popular in 19th-century English country gardens designed in the vernacular style.

Terraces & Tiers

The ziggurats of ancient Mesopotamia and the Hanging Gardens of Babylon are among the earliest recorded examples of terracing used in gardens. Later, terracing featured as a strong architectural element in Italian Renaissance and grand French gardens. Essentially a terrace is a flat platform for walking and viewing the garden. Usually constructed of hard materials such as stone paving, it extends from or is positioned close to the house. Often elevated, it may be arranged on several tiered levels that are connected by flights of stairs.

Powis Castle, Powys, Wales
Built to the highest standards (c.1680) and beset with fine sculpture, the visitor strolling these terraces might easily imagine him or herself to be in Italy, rather than mid-Wales.

Balustrade
A terrace is edged with either a low wall or a balustrade. Designs vary but the finest are constructed of stone uprights, known as balusters, which support a continuous ledge of coping. Bulbous-based balusters, such as these, are very common.

Design
In this example the balusters are set at a greater distance apart. Note how half balusters (in this case of a waisted design) have been used to edge the solid pier. These are used to terminate the balustrade and mark the position of the flight of steps.

Style

A terrace should be consistent with the
architectural style of the building it fronts.
This gothic-style design is continued in
the detailing of the finial. Other popular
designs are bucolic figurines and acorn-
shaped finials made of stone.

Detail

Running the length of a balustrade you will
often see rows of ornate urns and containers
filled with cascading flowers and foliage.
Incorporated into wide terraces you may
also find seats, niches for sculptures or even
small wall-mounted fountains.

Sweeping Stairways & Simple Steps

It is a rare garden that has a completely flat terrain, therefore steps and stairways are essential features for most. However, alongside the purely functional necessity of transporting the visitor from one level to another, stairs can provide a focal point of great pomp and grandeur. A wide variety of steps are integral to many features, for instance you will see them by terraces, as part of buildings such as temples and pavilions, inside towers and belvederes, alongside cascades, in sunken gardens, as well as inset into mounts and banks.

Steps that take note of practical considerations
A location with such unusually precipitous differences in level as this one requires not just well-built flights of steps but also strong retaining walls.

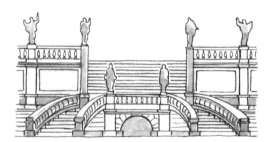

Ornament
Many of these great ornate staircases are embellished with expensive, finely detailed balustrading, columns and stonework. Note how some are also vehicles for displaying statuary while others contain integral fountains or semi-circular dipping wells.

Formal stairs
The architects of Italian Renaissance gardens made a virtue out of overcoming their hilly terrain by designing highly elaborate and complex flights of steps. Look for the numerous variations that exist based on the matrix of the symmetrical double staircase.

Random steps

At the other end of the scale you will find simple random stepping stones set directly into the ground. These may meander gently through more natural areas such as woodland gardens, or be used as improvised bridges to cross small streams.

Rustic steps

In wild or woodland gardens you will frequently find rustic steps made of earth and retained by split logs. These vary in width and may only be installed at particularly steep inclines. They are very effective while visually unobtrusive.

Up the Garden Path

Appropriate choice of paving
Large slabs of mellow stone laid in a random formation make one of the most visually sympathetic, and long lasting, of garden paths.

A path may be wide or narrow, straight or sinuous, constructed of hard materials or soft, the variations are almost infinite. In public gardens or parks the choice is likely to be dictated by the footfall through a given area, while in private gardens greater consideration can be given to pure aesthetics. Traditionally soft materials were favoured, such as crushed seashells, fine gravel and even cinders from the fire, kept in place by retaining edges formed of wooden planks or decorative tiles. Later, stone and brick paving became the material of choice.

Half-basketweave bond

Stone and brick paving is hard wearing but expensive and requires a skilled craftsman to lay it, especially in patterns such as this. Note the quality of brick used (colour and texture) and the complexity of design.

Herringbone

Bricks laid in this traditional herringbone pattern look particularly attractive over a large area, such as a terrace. Simpler designs work better for narrow paths, like those that edge formal flower beds or pools.

Mixed materials

Using a mixed palette of carefully chosen materials can give very effective results. Look out for harmonious pairings, such as this path of brick and pebbles. It creates an interesting yet hard-wearing surface, suitable for any area that sees heavy traffic.

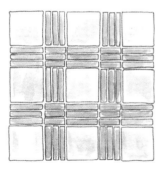

Texture

One of the most successful mixtures of materials you will see is the combination of terracotta tiles and cut tile ends. Much favoured by Arts and Crafts architects, these lovely textures grace many paths, low walls and flights of steps.

Building Bridges

A bridge is a functional means of crossing a stream, river or lake but in gardens a bridge's decorative contribution to the scene mostly outweighs any real practical purpose. Indeed those positioned in distant, rarely visited areas may be little more than eye-catchers. In more extreme cases you will see examples that are follies, such as the wooden bridge at Kenwood House, London, which is a mere façade! A consistent feature of oriental gardens, in Europe bridges were considered important in the 17th and 18th centuries, especially in large landscape gardens.

Monet-inspired garden
The Japanese-style bridge that the Impressionist artist Claude Monet (1840–1926) had built at his garden at Giverny, France, has many imitators the world over.

Japanese bridge
Extravagantly arched Japanese drum bridges, featured in the landscape prints of Ando Hiroshige (1797–1858), are made of wood, often red lacquer, with ornate latticework and finials. Their symbolic function is to link conceptually distinct areas of the Japanese garden. Far simpler slabs of granite are sometimes used to span smaller streams.

Chinese bridge
As well as spanning a stream or lake, the characteristic Chinese 'camel-back' bridge affords an elevated view of the surrounding scene. Made of brick or stone, often with carved balustrades, the semi-circular opening is high enough to allow small boats to pass beneath.

Palladian bridge

Among the grandest bridges you will see are those based on original designs by 16th-century Italian architect Andrea Palladio (1508–80) who designed the Rialto Bridge in Venice. These incorporate Classical features such as colonnades and pedimented archways, as in this example.

Rustic bridge

Bridge construction has often been seen as an opportunity to introduce playfulness or theatricality into the garden and rococo-, gothic- and Moorish-influenced designs are not uncommon. By contrast simple rustic bridges that were fashionable in the 19th century are still seen in country settings.

Rockeries

Rockwork is a traditional feature in Chinese and Japanese gardens and was used for Roman and later Renaissance grottoes. In Europe several 18th-century gardens introduced large arrangements of rocks intended to imitate picturesque scenes from nature. However, a totally new way of using rocks was developed in Victorian Britain. Rock gardens or rockeries, complex arrangements of imported rocks to create miniature mountainous scenes, are interplanted with small alpine and rock-loving species of plants. Still popular today, those on a grander scale often incorporate pools and rockwork bridges.

Rockery garden
The subtle use of rocks and plants blends well with the naturalistic planting of this garden. the arrangement appearing neither dominant nor insignificant.

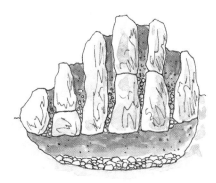

Construction

The best rockeries look completely natural but, as this cross-section diagram shows, they are constructed from varying sized rocks and rubble then infilled with soil for planting. The larger the rocks used, the more convincing the final result.

Strata

Look for rockeries where the visible faces of the rocks imitate geological strata. Delicate alpine plants can easily be overlooked when growing at ground level but this tiered effect allow the inspection of specimen plants at relatively close quarters.

Plants

It is essential to achieve a balance of plants and rocks: too many rockeries appear to be either all stone or all greenery. Alongside alpines you will see other plants incorporated such as ferns, spring bulbs and dwarf conifers.

Position

You will find many gardens have more subtle rockery-style areas rather than great freestanding outcrops of stone. Steps edged with rocks can look particularly successful, as do low walls constructed with pockets of soil established for plants.

Artificial Stonework

So great was the demand for architectural display features in gardens from the mid-18th century onwards that copies of Classical designs for ornaments such as statuary began to be manufactured in considerable quantities. Many of the finest examples you will see originated at Coade's Artificial Stone Manufactory, London. Opened in 1769 by Mrs Eleanor Coade, the work is characterised by particularly fine detailing. In 1848 the English landscape gardening firm of James Pulham and Son introduced its proprietary Pulhamite stone, an artificial cement-based compound of great verisimilitude.

Coade stone urn
Note the quality of the fine detailing on this Coade stone urn, one of several that grace the gardens at Hestercombe in Somerset, England.

Coade products
A great range of Coade stone items were produced during the life of the factory including memorials, coats of arms, statuary and countless large-scale urns and vases. Note the delicacy of the relief work on the stone column supporting this armillary sphere.

Coade stone
Mrs Coade's moulded artificial stone was a form of ceramic stoneware that was produced in great quantities (her daughter, also Eleanor, continued the business until 1813). Such is the quality that many examples still survive and are highly sought after.

Pulhamite stone

Many of the elaborate rockeries of Victorian Britain were constructed by the Pulhams (including those at Buckingham Palace, London and the gardens at Wisley, Surrey). Some are constructed using a mixture of natural and artificial stone, although it is very difficult to distinguish between them.

Pulhamite products

Pulhams' rockeries, ferneries, grottoes, caves and cascades were made from a base of bricks and rubble, covered with their particular mix of Portland stone cement, then coloured to reflect the natural stone found in the locality. Like Coade stone, Pulhamite is very long lasting.

The Birds & the Bees

Many gardens contain structures associated with the housing of various types of wildlife and domestic animals. Look out for stables (many later converted to garages as motor vehicles replaced horses), deer houses that are sometimes seen on grand estates and even fancy kennels, dovecotes, apiaries and aviaries are not uncommon. Extravagances such as highly ornate menageries, pheasantries and even model dairies have also been in vogue in various periods but few were long-lived. As these animal houses are classed as part of the working garden, most are unlikely to be found close to the main house.

Working harmony
Beehives are the perfect addition to vegetable, herb and fruit gardens as their industrious inhabitants are vital for the pollination of many crops.

Dovecote
Dating back to Roman times, the dovecote's most characteristic form is a round stone or brick tower with nest holes set high into the walls, each with a perch or shared ledge for alighting. Less substantial modern ones are often wooden and painted white.

Apiary
In gardens you may see individual hives, an apiary (area for keeping hives), a bee house (covered structure for sheltering hives) or a bee bole (an arched niche set into a wall to protect traditional bee-skeps, such as the one illustrated above).

Aviary

Like dovecotes, aviaries date from Roman times. They denoted great wealth during the medieval era and in later periods were used to display exotic species brought back from foreign travels. Their popularity then declined and many now lie empty.

Birdbath

Nowadays people prefer to observe birds flying free, nesting, feeding and drinking. To this end, many gardens contain a variety of nesting boxes, bird tables and feeders, and birdbaths. The latter are shallow basins usually mounted on a decorative base.

Art Outdoors

Sculptural forms are found in all types of garden, of varied design and located in many different situations. Some of the finest, and most elaborate, are the large-scale iconographic schemes that furnished the great Italian and French gardens from the Renaissance onwards. Here marble and bronze are the favoured materials. In northern European and American gardens examples are often more restrained and stone and lead more common (the tones more suited to the cooler light). In the modern period garden landscapes have often been adopted as appropriate settings in which to display contemporary works.

Sutton Place, Surrey, England
This sculpture by Ben Nicholson (1894–1982), known as the Nicholson Wall, provides the perfect focal point in the cerebral scheme designed by Geoffrey Jellicoe (1900–1996).

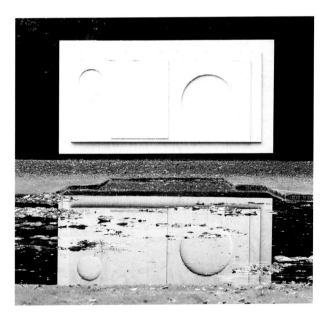

Position

Note where a sculpture has been placed: big statement pieces may terminate a vista, be positioned at the junction of an axis or provide an arresting focal point. More modest examples may be placed in intimate spaces and partially hidden by foliage.

Subject

Garden sculpture may depict unexpected subjects that bear little or no relation to their setting. Ask yourself whether this has been done for theatrical effect, whether it evokes a serious historical association, or is it simply a playful diversion?

Animals

Animals are enduringly popular subjects for sculptural features, and may be very grand (look for mythological creatures such as Chinese dragons, unicorns, griffins) or much more prosaic and naturalistic, such as beasts of the hunt or faithful pets.

Materials

Look carefully to see what a sculpture is made of. The finest are carved from marble. Bronze and lead pieces are often cast in multiples, as are those made of artificial stone or cement. Modern works are constructed from a host of materials.

Figures in the Landscape

**Sausmarez Manor
Art Park, Guernsey,
Channel Islands**
These modern
bronze figures,
reclining on a
simple stone slab,
set a relaxed mood
quite unlike that
which would be
induced by a
classical grouping.

Statuary, or figurative sculpture, dates back to ancient Greece and Rome and these works of art are among the finest (and most copied) examples ever created. Popular subjects include gods and goddesses (either singly or in groups), emperors (frequently portrait busts) and military heroes (often on horseback). You will encounter figurative works in all kinds of gardens, from the sombre and allegorical to the whimsical and amusing. The quality and choice of subject of these pieces sets the tone and mood of the garden in a way few other features can.

Allegory

Look for figures modelled on Classical examples that personify certain ideals or activities. Here the attributes of palette and paintbrush are clues to the viewer that this figure represents the art of Painting. Other popular figures in this genre are those of Music and Architecture.

Ornamentation

In grand garden schemes figurative groups embellish features like pools and fountains. Also look for narrative relief panels – perhaps a coat of arms, family motto or emblem – used as decoration on a range of items.

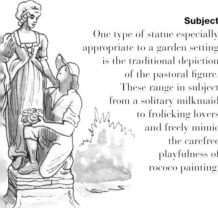

Subject

One type of statue especially appropriate to a garden setting is the traditional depiction of the pastoral figure. These range in subject from a solitary milkmaid to frolicking lovers and freely mimic the carefree playfulness of rococo painting.

Supports

Portrait busts are usually mounted on pedestals and columns, or may be set within arched or oval wall niches. A rectangular pillar (known as a herm) or a tapering version (term) support sculptures either of people, animals or mythical figures.

In Memoriam

Mausoleums, tombs and memorials commemorating the dead are sometimes seen in private gardens and public parks. One of the most famous, India's Taj Mahal (1654), is actually a Mughal tomb garden. Erecting memorials and shrines to national heroes and literary figures from the past became something of a vogue towards the end of the 18th century, especially in British gardens. The intention was to invoke in the viewer meditations on mortality. This tradition continues, as the Diana, Princess of Wales Memorial Fountain in London's Hyde Park illustrates.

Mausoleum, Bowood House, Wiltshire, England
This muscular building designed by Robert Adam (1728–1792) sets an appropriately sombre tone. It houses the tombs of the Lansdowne family.

Mausoleum
A mausoleum is a building for housing tombs, usually those of one family. The term can also refer to a single tomb. Redolent of dynastic display, and often monumental in scale, they may be positioned prominently in a landscape.

Statue
You will see statues commemorating often long-forgotten figures in public parks and gardens the world over. Mounted high on stately plinths these former civic notaries look down on formal flower gardens, fountains and disinterested passers-by.

Memorial

Memorial plaques may be simple wall-mounted tablets bearing an inscription, or more substantial freestanding monuments. The latter, often topped with cloth-draped funereal urns cast in stone, can commemorate events as well as people.

Animal graves

Tucked away in a quiet shady corner of a garden you may come across a haphazard group of small gravestones. Often just proclaiming a single name and a set of dates, these are poignant reminders of former much-loved pets.

Ornamental Urns & Vases

The terms urn and vase are often used interchangeably. Unlike plant containers, urns and vases are purely decorative features with no functional purpose, other than their occasional use as commemorative or memorial items. They vary in design and scale considerably and may be hollow, solid, open or have a closed top or lid. A particularly large example can provide a very effective focal point in a garden or, if mounted on a pedestal, terminate a vista. Other common locations are sitting atop balustrading or flanking flights of steps.

Simple and effective
This arrangement of fine pedestal-mounted urns, hedge and lawn is an exercise in restraint, the result equally effective throughout the seasons.

Materials

Urns and vases are high-status objects and most usually are made from lead, stone or terracotta (a fine quality earthenware that ages attractively over time). The lion's head and swag design on this lead urn is very typical of what you may see.

Design

The florid ornamentation of this vase is such that filling it with flowers and foliage would only detract from the striking shape of its silhouette. To achieve maximum impact an item like this requires careful positioning within the garden.

Pedestal

You will notice many urns and vases mounted on a pedestal as this increases the overall height and stature of the object. Often the urn and base has been conceived as a single design and both are equally decorative.

Grecian vase

Large stone Grecian-style vases, originally from Greece, Spain and Italy, provide striking focal points in many gardens. Although simpler in design than many urns and vases, their scale, rich colour and texture need no floral adornment.

Containers: the materials

Plant containers are essential components in many gardens around the world. Indeed in courtyard gardens they often provide the only means of growing plants and flowers. Materials range from the traditional, such as ceramic (either decorated with colourful glazes or unglazed), terracotta, stone or lead, to the more contemporary use of stainless steel or even fibreglass. The former age well and acquire a pleasing worn patina over time while the newer materials remain sharp and crisp to the eye. In the 19th century numerous cast iron containers were mass-produced even though this material is prone to rust.

Traditional container
Stone containers always lend an air of glamour and quality to a garden and are better suited to formal settings, such as within this box parterre.

Terracotta
Terracotta pots have been produced for thousands of years. Few materials are so sympathetic to the garden setting but it has disadvantages. Unglazed terracotta is porous so plants require frequent watering. Frost damage to the container is also a risk.

Stone
Stone, real or artificial, is commonly used for pots and you will see highly decorative pieces from many periods. Along with the actual container, there may be ornate pedestals and supports, such as this heavily burdened cherub.

Metal

Like terracotta and stone, metals such as lead, bronze and copper age beautifully in the garden. Look for recycled items such as water cisterns and old copper boilers now being used as attractive planters. Stainless steel is popular for contemporary designs.

Wood

Wood requires more maintenance than other materials and will eventually rot. Painting or treatment with preservative helps extend its life. Wooden containers make stylish, often quite large, cases for growing trees and shrubs.

Containers: the design

You will see literally hundreds of different designs for plant pots and containers in gardens but look out for recurring shapes. These traditional designs have withstood changes in fashion and often have been made for a specific purpose. Italian Renaissance gardens made great use of large-scale pots. These were strategically positioned as focal points, or several were arranged in rhythmic rows. Pots overflowing with foliage and flowers grace terraces, stairways and pool sides while the external appearance of the humblest dwelling is significantly enhanced by the simple addition of a window box or two.

Natural pairing
The simplicity of this collection of terracotta pots perfectly complements the rustic quality of this woven seat, their style and function in harmony.

Design

Deep, wide terracotta pots are traditionally used for growing citrus trees. Other types include those with apertures (for strawberries) and shallow half pans (for alpines). Tall, thin pots, known as Long Toms, encourage root development.

Trough

Rectangular troughs are often decorated with elaborate mouldings such as swags, bows, flowers, and may be raised off the ground on matching supports. A painted wooden box, with finials at the four corners, is known as a Versailles Case.

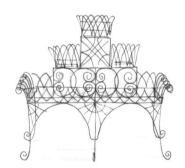

Jardinière

Occasionally you will see special stands designed to display several plants together in attractive trailing tiered arrangements. Typically made of ornate wrought iron, or wooden slats, they are popular for furnishing conservatories, winter gardens or the grander types of glasshouse.

Contemporary

Ask yourself if container and planting are suited and whether they sit well in their surroundings. Modern gardens often require strong architectural shapes and slick materials such as stainless or galvanised steel while containers of strong colour need careful placing.

Places of Repose

As many gardens are primarily sites of pleasure, play and enjoyment, it is natural that they should be fully furnished for the comfort of their inhabitants. Rare is the garden that contains no shady seat or bench from which to enjoy a prospect. As with other architectural features, garden furniture has been subject to changing fashion and periodic revivals. Note whether a piece of furniture has been chosen for effect, comfort or both (inviting recliners are likely to be favoured in domestic gardens over formal wrought iron chairs).

The unexpected
Look out for novelty designs such as this delightful swan seat! As one of the more ephemeral garden features seating is often an opportunity to introduce a flight of fancy.

Position
The garden bench is found in almost all types of gardens. This simple seat is a stalwart of public parks and gardens the world over. When carefully positioned it marks a natural resting point (both physically and visually) in a landscape.

Style
Ideally the style of furniture should reflect that of the garden. The British 19th-century craze for all things gothic led to the mass production of elaborate cast-iron tables, chairs and benches, destined for middle-class gardens and gothic-style conservatories.

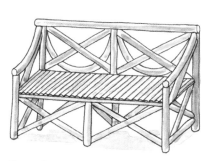

Materials

Unpainted hardwood has an affinity with any outdoor setting and its appearance usually improves with time. Oak, for instance, turns silver. Simple designs work almost anywhere; more fanciful rustic styles continue to be popular in country gardens.

Novelty

Endless invention has characterised the design of garden furniture. Swinging seats on strong supports add an air of jollity and playfulness and are usually best placed to enjoy lovely views. Some have brightly coloured awnings for shade.

Garden Furniture

In keeping with its sometimes innovative design, an imaginative range of materials is also often used to construct garden furniture. Alongside the hard-wearing and heavy-duty staples such as stone, wood and metal, far more delicate effects are achieved using lighter weight substances like fine wrought iron. Furniture made from various types of wickerwork always sits happily in garden and conservatory. This ancient technique involves plaiting or weaving together fine strands of twigs, cane, willow, rush etc. to form surprisingly strong items of furniture.

The garden terrace
Wrought iron produces furniture of great delicacy of design while also being strong and durable. The material suits a range of garden settings.

Simple bench

The Italian Renaissance bench is among the finest of garden furniture. A cool marble slab, supported on hand-carved trestles, it has few rivals. Unfortunately poor stone and concrete cast versions abound, often sited inappropriately.

Barrow seat

Practical and fun. much as its name suggests the barrow seat can be wheeled from place to place in the garden. just like a wheelbarrow. It allows the restless garden visitor to seek sun or shade. peace or diversion.

Rusticity

You occasionally find natural features made into furniture. like this old tree being used for a table base. Akin to stumperies and root houses, such rusticity is the antithesis of formal garden furniture and seeks to blur the line between the garden and nature.

Tree seat

Another attempt to bring people and nature closer together is the delightful notion of a tree seat. Rather like a tree house. the sitter enjoys the sensation of being surrounded by the tree. along with practicalities such as shade and comfort.

Marking Time

Instruments such as sundials, armillary spheres and weathervanes make attractive additions to many gardens. Records of sundials date back to *c.*1500 BC and armillary spheres to *c.*250 BC. Now their original functions are largely redundant they are used as decorative architectural features, providing small-scale focal points. Quiet contemplation of a sundial can evoke in the viewer meditations on the passing of time and musings on human mortality. Inscriptions are often integral to their design: at Rudyard Kipling's garden, Bateman's, in Sussex, England, the sundial bears the legend 'It is later than you think'.

Celestial centrepiece
An armillary sphere provides a light and airy centrepiece to this formal garden, its position echoed in the heavier ornate urn beyond.

Sundial

A sundial utilises the shadow of the sun to tell the time. The dial face (commonly bronze) is marked with the hours while the upright (gnomon) casts the shadow. It must be carefully positioned in relation to the celestial pole and to latitude.

Design

Sundials vary in design and can be mounted horizontally on a pedestal or vertically on a wall. Ornately carved supports may feature allegorical figures such as Father Time. They must, of course, be sited in full sun, and traditionally were surrounded by formal rose gardens.

Armillary sphere

Armillary spheres are constructed of connected concentric metal rings. These are an astronomical representation of the celestial globe. In a garden setting you will find them mounted on a pedestal. Especially suited to smaller gardens, they make striking focal points.

Weathervane

Characterised by compass points and a variety of decorative figures, the spinning weathervane indicates the direction and, sometimes, speed of the wind. They top many types of buildings including those in gardens. Their American cousins are the wooden carved figures known as whirligigs.

APPENDICES

Glossary

ALLEY a long formal walk in a garden, often edged by trees. The term also refers to narrow lawn for ball games.

AMPHITHEATRE an open area, typically circular with raised seating, devoted to outdoor performances.

ANNUAL a plant that only lives for a year or less.

APIARY area for keeping bee hives.

ARBORETUM a collection of different species of trees. *See also* **PINETUM**.

ARBOUR a small shelter open at the top and sides, usually containing a seat. Also known as a bower.

ARCADE a series of linked arches, usually architectural but may be made of hedging plants.

ARCHITECTURAL PLANTS a term used to refer to plants that are prized for the strong form of their foliage, rather than their flowers.

ARMILLARY SPHERE an astronomical representation, usually made of metal, of the celestial globe.

AVIARY Large cages for housing birds.

AVENUE A long, straight walk or drive lined with evenly spaced trees or sometimes clipped hedging.

BALUSTRADE a parapet formed of a row of balusters topped with a rail, often constructed from stone and used to edge a terrace.

BANQUETING HOUSE a building, separate from the main house, positioned in a garden used for formal eating and drinking.

BARROW SEAT a bench or seat with a wheel at one end, like a wheelbarrow.

BASIN a simple shallow bowl, often mounted on a pedestal.

BASTION an elevated walkway that ends in a vantage point.

BEDDING PLANTS plants raised to plant out for a short seasonal display. Often they are tender annuals and form part of a decorative scheme.

BEE BOLE an arched niche set into a wall to protect traditional bee skeps from the weather.

BELL-JAR a glass cover used for protecting young and tender plants.

BELT a broad planting of trees, often found at the perimeter of an estate.

BELVEDERE a high structure, such as a tower, from which to enjoy a view.

BOATHOUSE a building positioned alongside a lake or river for housing boats.

BOG GARDEN a collection of plants suited to growing in the soft, marshy ground found at the edges of ponds.

BORROWED VIEW an attractive scene that exists outside the perimeter of a garden but one that is enjoyed from within.

BOSCO a small wood.

BOSQUET a shrubbery or dense planting of trees.

BOTANIC GARDEN a large collection of plants intended for scientific study and display, usually with public access.

BOTHY a simple building located within a garden for housing young gardeners.

BOWER *see* **ARBOUR**.

CANAL an artificial stretch of flat, still water.

CARPET BED flowering and foliage plants densely planted together in a pattern and cut into a lawn or flat area such as gravel.

CASCADE an arrangement of falling water, may be natural or an architectural construction driven by a pump.

CATENARY method of growing flowering plants, often roses, on a rope slung between two posts.

CHARBAGH an enclosed Islamic garden with pools of water that are symbolic of the four rivers of life.

CLEARING an open area of ground found within a wood.

CLAIRVOYEE an ornate ironwork panel set within a wall or sometimes a hedge to provide a view.

CLOCKHOUSE a building that displays a clock face on its façade; sometimes more than one is shown.

CLOISTER an enclosed garden within a monastery or convent.

CLOSE BOARD FENCE a solid fence constructed of boards with no gaps in between.

CLUMP a group of trees planted together.

COADE STONE a type of artificial stone named after its creator, Mrs Eleanor Coade.

COLD FRAME a brick or wooden box with removable glazed panels, used for acclimatising young or tender plants before planting out in the ground.

COLONNADE a regularly spaced single row of columns, often running parallel with a wall to form a corridor.

COLUMN a tall, narrow pillar, which may form part of an architectural scheme such as a building, or be freestanding. *See also* **ORDER**.

CONSERVATORY a glazed structure attached to a building. Although plants are commonly displayed here they are primarily intended for the comfort of people and are usually well furnished.

COPING the capping at the top of a wall.

COPPICE a managed wood or area in which trees are cut to the ground every few years, encouraging tall and slender new growth from the stump. The shoots produced by coppicing were, in centuries past, an important resource with various uses.

CRINKLE-CRANKLE WALL an undulating, curved wall, often used for growing fruit; also known as a serpentine wall.

DECIDUOUS the term for plants that shed their leaves each autumn.

DIPPING POOL or **WELL** originally a pool for filling up watering cans or buckets. Later they became decorative features, often circular and set into a wall.

DOVECOTE a structure for housing doves.

DRUM BRIDGE a particularly rounded style of bridge, often seen in Chinese gardens.

ESPALIER a fruit tree trained into a geometric shape.

EVERGREEN the term for plants that retain their leaves all year round.

EXEDRA a semi-circular backdrop arranged like the apse in a church.

EXOTIC a plant that is not native to the country in which it is growing.

EYE-CATCHER any noticeable feature that attracts attention.

FERNERY a collection of ferns.

FESTOON *see* **CATENARY**.

FOLLY a garden structure that lacks a function and is just for effect.

FORCER a tall terracotta pot with an open bottom and lidded top. It is placed over certain plants such as rhubarb to obscure daylight and 'force' the growth.

FORCING PIT area for forcing fruit.

FORMAL refers to a regular and ordered style of garden layout and planting.

FRUTICETUM a collection of shrubs.

GALLERY an arrangement of multiple arches made from a light framework of iron or wood and covered with climbing plants.

GARDEN ROOM a generic term for any room either in a garden or attached to a house that overlooks the garden.

GATEHOUSE a building positioned at the entrance to a property and occupied by a gatekeeper whose job is to monitor visitors.

GAZEBO originally a small elevated structure from which to view a garden, now used to refer to various garden structures that contain a seat.

Glossary

GAZON COUPÉ a pattern cut into turf and filled with sand or gravel.

GIARDINO SEGRETO a secret enclosed garden.

GIOCHI D'ACQUA literally a water joke, usually involving an element of surprise (and often a wetting!) for anyone in the vicinity.

GLASSHOUSE a glazed building for displaying plants; usually more ornate than a greenhouse.

GREENHOUSE a glazed building for raising plants.

GROTTO a cave-like construction, usually made of rock and stone, which may be natural or artificial.

GROVE a small ornamental wood.

HA-HA a steep ditch that keeps grazing animals out of a garden without the need of a visual boundary.

HAND-LIGHT glass panes set into a frame that is used to cover young plants for protection from the weather.

HEDGE shrubby plants planted in a line and cut to a uniform height.

HERBACEOUS BORDER a border planted with herbaceous plants. Also known as a perennial border.

HERBACEOUS PLANT a perennial plant that dies back in winter.

HERBAL a book devoted to the uses of herbal plants.

HERBARIUM a collection of plants that have been preserved by drying or pressing.

HERM a rectangular pillar topped with a sculpture of a person, animal or mythical creature.

HERMITAGE an abode used by a hermit, usually very roughly constructed.

HORTUS CONCLUSUS literally an enclosed garden, it came to be associated with Christian religious symbolism.

ICE HOUSE a stone or brick structure packed with ice and used for preserving foodstuffs.

INFORMAL refers to an irregular and naturalistic style of garden layout and planting.

ISLAND BED a freestanding bed cut into a lawn and planted with shrubs and flowers.

ITALIANATE the use of Italian architectural features in other countries.

KIOSK a small garden shelter built in a variety of exotic styles.

KITCHEN GARDEN an area of garden devoted to the cultivation of edible plants.

KNOT GARDEN a decorative arrangement of low-growing clipped hedges, either left open or filled with plants.

LABYRINTH a pattern arranged on the ground with a single path. May be two-dimensional, such as a design cut into grass or three-dimensional – for example, constructed of hedging.

LAWN an area of mown grass.

LAYERING a method of weaving and pruning a hedge to encourage thick growth.

LODGE a small dwelling positioned at the entrance to an estate.

LOGGIA a row of columns or uprights forming a cloister or arcade. It has a solid roof, is attached to a building and open at one side.

LYCH GATE a gateway covered by a substantial roof. Some may include rudimentary seating.

MARGINAL a plant that grows in the boggy soil at the edges of ponds.

MAZE a complex pattern delineated by hedging with many blind alleys and dead ends. *See also* **LABYRINTH**.

MEADOW an area of grasses and other plants managed by a regime that involves cutting at certain times of the year. Meadows may also be managed by grazing animals, which are then periodically removed to give preference to certain plants, often flowering ones.

MAUSOLEUM a building for housing tombs. The term may also refer to a single tomb.

MOAT an area of water around a building, originally for defensive purposes.

MOON GATE a circular aperture set within a wall in Chinese gardens.

MOSSERY a collection of mosses.

MOUND/MOUNT a hill-like shape in a garden, often manmade.

NATIVE a plant which naturally occurs in a particular region.

NICHE a recessed area in a wall or sometimes in a clipped hedge for displaying sculpture.

NUTTERY a collection of nut trees.

NYMPHAEUM a place where offerings were made to nymphs in Ancient Greece.

OBELISK a tapering pillar, may be four-sided, triangular, circular or octagonal.

ORANGERY a substantial roofed building for housing tender citrus trees in winter.

ORDER the form and decoration used for columns based on Classical Greek and Roman models.

PAGODA a tall, tiered building based on traditional Chinese designs.

PALM HOUSE a glasshouse used for the cultivation and display of palm trees and other exotic species.

PARTERRE a decorative bed designed to be viewed from above.

PARTERRE À L'ANGLAISE A design cut into a lawn.

PARTERRE DE BRODERIE a design based on elaborate embroidery patterns.

PARTERRE DE COMPARTIMENT a design that is symmetrical horizontally and vertically.

PARTERRE D'EAU a design made from pools of water.

PATTE D'OIE a formal planting of trees arranged in the shape of a goose's foot.

PAVILION a garden building that provides shelter and shade.

PEDIMENT a gable positioned above a portico or above a door or window.

PERGOLA a series of upright pillars or columns supporting cross beams used for growing climbing plants.

PERENNIAL a long-lived plant that dies back in winter. *See also* **HERBACEOUS BORDER.**

PHYSIC GARDEN a garden devoted to the growing of medicinal herbs and plants.

PICKET FENCE a regular wooden fence formed from uprights and rails.

PINERY a glasshouse used for growing pineapples.

PINETUM a collection of coniferous trees.

PLEACHING the technique of pruning a tree to produce a single tall trunk with the upper branches trained horizontally to appear like a hedge on a pole.

PLEASURE GARDEN/GROUND a large-scale garden used for public entertainments such as musical performances, games and promenading.

POLLARD this technique involves cutting the top of the tree trunk each year, encouraging multiple stems to sprout.

POOLHOUSE a building positioned near a swimming pool and used for changing.

POTAGER an ornamental vegetable or kitchen garden.

PRAIRIE a style of planting characterised by large drifts of late-flowering perennials and grasses.

PULHAMITE a type of artificial stone made by James Pulham and Son.

QUINCUNX a group of five trees planted in the shape that represents the number five on a die. The formation may be repeated.

RAISED BED a contained bed for growing plants that is elevated above the ground.

Glossary

RIBBON BED a long, narrow border with continuous strips of brightly coloured low growing plants.

RILL a small stream or brook, often straight and edged with stone.

ROCK GARDEN or **ROCKERY** an arrangement of rocks inset with pockets of soil for growing plants.

ROOT HOUSE a hut constructed from giant tree roots.

ROSARY/ROSARIUM a rose garden.

ROTUNDA a circular ring of columns with a domed roof, which may be open-sided or enclosed.

RUIN a building or structure in a semi-ruined state; may be a fragment of an earlier structure or intentionally constructed this way.

RUSTIC a style of building and making that is usually associated with the country and is characterised by rough, rather crude materials and finishes.

SERPENTINE LAKE an irregularly shaped area of water with a curving and sinuous edge.

SERPENTINE WALL see **CRINKLE-CRANKLE**.

SHRUBBERY a group of densely planted woody and flowering shrubs.

STANDARD a shrub, such as a rose, grown as a tree with a single stem, may be grafted onto stock from another type of plant.

STUMPERY a group of old uprooted tree stumps arranged as a decorative feature.

SUMMERHOUSE a garden building used to provide shelter and shade.

SUNDIAL a device that uses the shadow of the sun to tell the time.

SUNK GARDEN a garden created in a depression in the ground.

TEAHOUSE a traditional building used for the performance of the tea ceremony in Japanese gardens.

TEATRO DI VERDURA Italian term for an open air theatre.

TEMPLE a roofed building, may be open at the sides or enclosed.

TERM a tapering rectangular pillar topped with a sculpture of a person, animal or mythical creature.

TERRACOTTA a fine quality earthenware used for making plant pots, containers and statues.

THICKET a tightly planted group of trees.

TOPIARY the art of clipping plants into ornamental shapes.

TREE SEAT a seat constructed around the trunk of a tree.

TRELLISWORK openwork wooden fencing, often very decorative.

TROUGHERY a group of troughs, often made of stone, containing plants.

URN a decorative vase, may have an open or closed top.

VASE a decorative vessel.

VINERY a glasshouse used for growing grapes.

VISTA a long-distance view, often with a focal point.

VITICETUM a collection of vines.

WEATHERVANE a decorative device that shows the points of the compass and indicates the direction of the wind.

WELLHEAD a device constructed over a well for drawing water.

WELLHOUSE a building constructed over a wellhead.

WHIRLIGIG an American term for a carved wooden figure used much like a weathervane.

WICKERWORK material made by weaving or plaiting fine strands of twigs, cane, willow, rush etc, often used for garden furniture.

WINTER GARDEN a large glasshouse used for public entertainment where plants were originally displayed.

Resources

UK & Europe

THE NATIONAL TRUST, founded in 1895, protects special places in England, Wales and Northern Ireland, many of which have equally special gardens to visit. www.nationaltrust.org.uk

Scotland and the Republic of Ireland have their own National Trusts: the National Trust for Scotland, www.nts.org/uk and An Taisce, the National Trust for Ireland. www.antaisce.org

THE NATIONAL GARDENS SCHEME (NGS), founded in 1927, has opened normally private gardens to the public a few days each year to raise funds for nursing and caring charities. THE YELLOW BOOK is an annual listing of over 3,700 private gardens including allotments open for this purpose. www.ngs.org.uk

ROYAL HORTICULTURAL SOCIETY (RHS) One of the world's leading horticultural organisations dedicated to advancing horticulture and promoting good gardening through events and annual shows such as the Chelsea Flower Show and the Hampton Court Flower Show. In addition to the four gardens owned by the RHS in the UK, the society has links with selected private gardens throughout the UK and in France, Belgium, Italy and North America. Its website lists 147 RHS-recommended gardens in the UK and 23 overseas that are open without charge to its members. www.rhs.org.uk

BOTANIC GARDENS CONSERVATION INTERNATIONAL (BGCI) This organisation brings together botanic gardens to work for plant conservation through science, education and horticulture. The website provides contacts in botanic garden and plant conservation networks throughout Europe. www.bgci.org

North America

THE GARDEN CLUB OF AMERICA (GCA) This umbrella organisation for US and Canadian local garden clubs was set up in 1923 to stimulate the knowledge and love of gardening. It offers awards and scholarships for graduate studies related to the protection of the environment. Its sites list botanical gardens and arboreta as well as links to specific societies and other GCA club websites. www.gcamerica.org

Publications

Gardens of the National Trust
STEPHEN LACEY
(National Trust, 2005)

The Gardens of Europe: A Traveller's Guide
CHARLES QUEST-RITSON
(Garden Art Press, 2007)

Gardens in France
ANGELIKA TASCHEN, DEIDI VON SCHAEWEN and MARIE-FRANÇOISE VALÉRY
(Taschen, 2008)

Gardens of Italy
ANN LARÅS
(Frances Lincoln, 2005)

Gardens of Portugal
HELENA ATTLEE
(Frances Lincoln, 2007)

In Search of Paradise: Great Gardens of the World
PENELOPE HOBHOUSE
(Frances Lincoln, 2006)

Index

Index

Acknowledgements

AUTHOR ACKNOWLEDGEMENTS

Many thanks to all at Ivy Press for their help, support and encouragement, especially Stephanie Evans, Jason Hook, Caroline Earle, Michael Whitehead, Katie Greenwood and Peter Bridgewater. What a team!

Special thanks to Juliet Nicolson for writing such a special introduction.

A big thank you goes to Coral Mula for her lovely illustrations and for being so unfailingly efficient.

Lastly can I thank all the garden owners and their tireless gardeners (who are often one and the same) who toil in wonderful gardens, grand and small, private and public, then generously throw open their gates and allow the likes of me inside to visit. It is always a privilege.

PICTURE CREDITS

The publisher would like to thank the following individuals and organisations for their kind permission to reproduce the images in this book. Every effort has been made to acknowledge the pictures, however we apologise if there are any unintentional omissions.

Garden Picture Library:
Leroy Alfonse: 84; Matt Anker: 194; Peter Baistow: 126; Lucy Barden: 60; Richard Bloom: 98; Mark Bolton: 68, 73BR, 80, 106, 131, 174, 206; Clive Boursnell: 48, 128, 147, 226; Lynne Brotchie: 17TR; Linda Burgess: 47BL; David Burton: 197T, 232; Brian Carter: 96; Michael Davis: 95BL; François De Heel: 118; Henk Dijkman: 169; David Dixon: 46, 94, 116, 141, 182, 199; Carole Drake: 89, 112, 132, 167TL, 197B; Ron Evans: 127TL; Richard Felber: 2, 44, 120, 127, 150, 153, 240; John Ferro Sims: 210; Nigel Francis: 47TL; Suzie Gibbons: 181, 185, 236; John Glover: 17TL, 57, 167BL, 167BR; Anne Green-Armytage: 209; Juliet Greene: 47TR; David Henderson: 200; Jacqui Hurst: 111, 186; Jason Ingram: 73TR, 179, 223, 228; Buro Kloeg/Niels Kooijman 134; Michèle Lamontagne: 124; J. Paul Moore: 167TR; Mayer/Le Scanff: 29; Martine Mouchy: 72; Clive Nichols: 47, 70, 170, 235, 242, 95TL; Cora Niele: 123, 137; Clay Perry: 63, 196R, 215; Howard Rice: 188, 203, 219, 225; Craig Roberts: 90, 197C; Ellen Rooney: 104, 160; Rosalind Simon: 86; Ron Sutherland: 163; Brigitte Thomas: 108; Mark Turner: 127BL; Michel Viard: 66; Juliette Wade: 196L; Lee Anne White: 92; Jo Whitworth: 95BR; Steven Wooster: 24, 100, 166; Francesca Yorke: 22

Paul MaCrae: 33

Photolibrary:
Dr Wilfried Bahnmüller: 26; Lee Beel: 36; Britain On View: 58, 138; Alberto Campanile: 144; Jonathan Carlile: 159; Angelo Cavalli: 204; David Clapp: 73TL; Corbis: 77; Carole Drake: 231; Dreamtours: 173; Chad Ehlers: 16; Nigel Francis: 74; John Glover: 127TR; Ips Co Limited: 193; The Irish Image Collection: 20, 142, 176, 216; Jumping Rocks: 64; Corinne Korda: 239; Georgianna Lane: 115; David Messent: 8; MiRa MiRa: 30; National Trust Photo Library: 83, 148; Andrew Newey: 14; Michael Newton: 51; Kevin O'Hara: 154; Paroligalperti: 95TR; Pawel Libera: 156; Pepeira Tom: 43; Pixtal: 40; Roy Rainford: 54; Mattes René: 19; Thomas Robbin: 190; Guido Alberto Rossi: 39; Claire Takacs: 73BL; Curtice Taylor: 220; Mark Turner: 17; John Warburton-Lee: 213; Barry Winiker: 11, 34; Koji Yamashita: 52; Ypps Ypps: 164

Nicola Stratford: 103